The Disorganised Business Owner's Bible

*The ultimate guide to a foolproof marketing machine
for any business regardless of niche, industry or location*

Ben Waters

Published by
SS1 Creative
www.ss1creative.com

First Edition published 2019

Contents

Preface

I'm going to keep this short. This book is for business owners who are looking to grow their business. It's as simple as that. Having read many business and 'self-help' books myself, I know just how important it is to skip the waffle.

I've called this the *Disorganised Business Owner's Bible* for a very specific reason. I'm sure you can guess part of it. Almost all my life I've been one of the most disorganised people I know. The trouble with being disorganised is, you can be very, very good at what you do, but on the outside appear useless.

As a person, I don't actually like being disorganised. And it's probably not the right word for it, although it's what people *perceive*. You see, having a very good upbringing, with parents and grandparents who reinforced rules, patience, respect and more – and attending a very good grammar school, theoretically I should be extraordinarily disciplined.

And maybe I'm hard on myself sometimes, but I think you *should* be hard on yourself. It's the only way you'll improve. Despite my failures, I've still written multiple books, countless guides and built a business that employs multiple staff. Sure, my successes could be greater, but each of us will take a unique path to our 'end goal'.

I went through a phase over a couple of years where, truth be told, I didn't really know how to deal with the growth of the business. We had a lot of sales thrust upon us very fast, and ultimately whether I succeeded or failed as a business owner depended on how I dealt with that work.

After all, if you do a great job, you might get a recommendation. If you do a terrible job, you'll definitely get a bad reputation. It was around the time I'd gone to see Dan Kennedy (a legend within the marketing world) and I'd been doing a hell of a lot of marketing.

I won't bore you with the details, but ultimately the failures came because we didn't have enough systems and procedures in place. We didn't have enough quality control. We didn't have enough project management. And quite frankly we didn't have enough highly talented staff.

Had I succeeded, this book may not have even been written. But I have no regrets. I wouldn't change the path I've been on because it's led me to where I am.

The contents of this book is, more or less, a summary of 'what was missing'. Things like, for example, how to build a proper marketing strategy *and* how to implement it. But something else I've done a lot of (obviously) over the last ten years, is build websites. Building a website can be a very simple, quick and easy job.

In fact I get people all the time, tell me how they couldn't possibly justify our fees for a website because they can do it themselves in an online builder. Just because the website looks pretty, doesn't make it a website that'll generate you leads and sales.

With that being said, let's get down to business.

Chapter One:
Introduction

There are thousands, upon thousands of business books out there. There are thousands, upon thousands of 'gurus' and 'experts' offering you some sort of advice. And it seems today, as if there are thousands more than there were, say, just ten years ago.

That's partly because of the obvious - it's been ten years... but I think it's significantly higher than, say, the previous ten years to that, because more and more people are now accepting that writing a book is one of the best ways to market yourself, and your business.

The clear question that arises is: "What makes this book any different, and perhaps more importantly, why should I trust you?"

As for the latter question, well, you shouldn't. Not yet.

The whole *point* of this book, is to give you information to allow you to test things for yourself, see them work, and grow your business... and *that* builds the trust. Or, you can see what I'm saying makes so much sense (and you can see why it works) that the trust builds from there.

As for what makes this book different... well, that's a tricky one. You see, marketing is marketing is marketing... and as long as you've got a marketing book from a <u>competent</u> and <u>experienced</u> author, then the only thing that makes this book different is... me.

It's completely filled with my own personality, my own stories, and my own opinions. You're getting my voice, my viewpoints, and my experience.

I've written this book because I want to help you.

Specifically, I want to help you grow your business, generate more leads and more sales, with less stress and fewer headaches. Sounds magical, but as I'm sure you know, it's actually a lot of hard work. There is no magic pill, and there is no overnight fix (with the exception of winning the lottery). Anyone that tries to convince you otherwise is someone to be very, very cautious of (I've met enough of them to know).

The tips and tricks in this book that I'll be sharing with you, *will* help you grow your business, and more importantly will help you grow your business if you don't know what day of the week it is half the time.

I've written this book specifically to help people like me. I've written it for the business owner that knows their business/trade damn well, but seem to get lumbered with so many jobs the important ones seem to fall to the back burner, until they become urgent, and then they're urgent *and* important – and that makes them even harder to deal with.

My point is, if you don't have the knowledge that I'm about to impart, you would *definitely* have more headaches and more stress trying to implement by yourself... but, am I the only one with this knowledge? Am I the only one to write a book on this subject? Of course not.

The reason I know these tricks and tips will help you (if you implement them) is because these are the very things that I do within my own business, and for my clients, that help us generate a constant stream of (often substantial) sales.

These are the things that I've taken over ten years to implement in my own business, but actually, I could have implemented ten years ago... had I found the right book.

So, read this book.

Read it, and implement. Please, implement.

For many of the techniques/tactics I will talk about, there's little to no cost involved, and that subsequently means no risk to you.

And if there's no risk to you, the only thing involved is... effort.

If you really want to grow your business, you've really not got anything to lose, except a bit of time and a bit of effort... but you've got everything to gain. Sounds a good deal, considering the upside is, that your business starts to generate a new constant stream of leads and sales.

Before we actually get going, and before you actually get knee deep in marketing, there's a question to ask.

An important question. It's a simple enough question...What do you want?

What's Your Goal?

Where do you want to be in 3 years? Is it a financial goal? A business goal? A life goal? A bit of all three?

The thing is, without the right focus and the right goals, and without *wanting* to actually achieve those goals, you're not going to progress any further than where you are now.

I've worked with a number of business coaches and mentors over the years, and they've all had various strategies and methods for growing your business.

The thing is many of them are so 'wrong' for my personality that it's a wonder I even began a conversation with them in the first place, let alone paid them ridiculous sums of money. My point here is, you've got to find a way of growing your business that revolves around the sort of person you are: Don't let people try to change your core personality.

Sure, you've probably got to make some changes to grow your business, and you'll have to go through some 'uncomfortable' change, but that's not to say you have to sacrifice what makes you 'you'.

Now, what are the key elements of a successful business?

What should you be aiming for?

If you've got staff, but the business still depends on you... whether you've got three, five or even ten staff, if the business is *completely* dependent on *your* actions day to day, then you've not got a 'business' as such, you've just created a company with a job for yourself.

Now I know that's a bit ridiculous.

My business is dependent on me still, but of course I classify it as a business (and it is). I'm forever working towards 'sacking myself'. I'm forever trying to remove myself from the critical operations of the company, because without doing so, I don't have a business, I just have a job. In fact, it's worse than that, because I don't have the *benefits* of a job.

Like knowing you're going to get paid at the end of the month. Like being able to just go home for the weekend and not stress about what jobs are coming in. Being able to switch off at night and not worry about the number of leads being a bit too low for this time of year.

Now I'm not going to sit here and tell you how to become the perfect business owner, because I'm far from that... but I know there's one thing that you <u>do</u> need to do, to achieve that true 'business'. That business where you're not needed every day, or any day.

That one thing you need to do, is to create a series of systems and procedures, so that your business can automatically run without you. It's *designed* to run without you.

There are many, many books out there which are more appropriate to talk you through this subject, and I'll recommend in the back of this book in my "Recommended Reading" section.

However, the systems I <u>can</u> talk to you about, because I've had a great deal of experience implementing for myself and for my clients, is a lead generation system.

This is, as it sounds, but it's one of the first pieces of the puzzle when it comes to breaking free from your business.

Because one of the biggest worries business owners always have is: "Where's the next sale coming from?"

Imagine, you set up a system that sends emails over the course of 2-3 months, runs Webinars, sends sales letters, schedules phone calls, etc.

And then imagine, that these emails, webinars and letters were all engineered to move someone closer to being a customer. By the time they've come to actually speak to you, they're at least 80% of the way to becoming a client.

And then imagine that you have automated systems bringing people to your website(s), and that a percentage of those people convert to leads, and a percentage of those people convert to clients.

There are many systems you can use that give you this sort of functionality, I use a combination of many... and I'll discuss all that in more detail in a bit.

So with all that in mind, *what's your goal?* To get your business independent from you? To build an automated marketing system? To have a constant stream of new business?

It's All About Your Mindset

Back when I first started getting serious about my business, I started exploring the 'business mentors' out there. I was recommended someone, and I checked out their stuff.

He was one of the leading 'info marketers' out there back in 2007. That is to say back then, his business was only to provide information on how to market your business.

Until that point, I had simply thought of marketing as advertising, but obviously it's just so much more than that. He would run seminars and had all sorts of other products etc, so I thought I'd see what my friend (who had recommended him to me) was doing with his material, and if they were going to purchase anything else from him.

But alas, my friend had taken little action... and the thing I noted was that he'd decided not to do anything else with the material, or buy any additional material, on the basis that all the marketer sells is 'mindset'.

But the thing is, it <u>starts</u> with mindset.

Because, without the right mindset, *this* whole book is useless to you. If you don't think certain things are going to be possible, your mind will argue with itself over every decision you take to improve your business, and subsequently you won't end up taking action on a lot of the things you should take action on.

Here's a good example. A few years back I changed our phone system at work. I'd had the same system since, well, as long as I can remember, definitely well over 10 years.

I'd decided, through sheer pig-headed mindset, that it was impossible to change our system. It was what it was, and nothing could be done about it. It was complicated. It was bespoke. It was ... blah blah blah.

Then, as I was about to train a member of staff on how to maintain it (because I was in the process of removing myself from that role), I noticed that our server was being 'brute forced' by a foreign IP address...

That is to say, someone was trying a lot of passwords very quickly for one of our extensions.

Now there are a multitude of ways around this, but I decided to put in a call to our hosting supplier to say "hey, blacklist this IP please".

As we got talking, turns out, they supplied VoIP services, and through nothing but a sheer bit of jiggery-pokery, within half an hour we'd changed phone systems.

Seriously.

It was that easy.

I'll be honest, I was pretty shocked, that I'd put up with a mediocre system for so long, and what's worse (well, better, I guess?) their service was cheaper.

Now, deep down, deep deep down... I'm a Windows man.

I grew up with Microsoft (well, a little fling with OS/2 Warp but we'll sidestep that for the moment).

From Windows 3.1 to Windows 10, I was a loyal and avid follower. I loved Windows Phone, I loved the Surface, I loved all things Microsoft.

And I put up with the stuff crashing because I thought "that's the way it is".

You know what I mean, right?

You click in a browser and you get the spinning wheel of doom or it goes white, then it carries on.

You go to save a document and it crashes; most of the time it's auto-saved but sometimes it just screws you enough to curse Microsoft all the way to hell and back.

But I put up with it. Because that's the way it was.

Then one day I'd had enough.

My PC crashed, and it looked like I'd completely lost everything. A helpful friend commented "At least you have everything backed up, right??"

It just so happened I got it all back, but even if it was backed up properly, it's not the point. The point was, I was plagued by issues.

I got angry.

With my PC unresponsive, I jumped in the car and drove to the nearest computer shop, and bought myself a MacBook Pro.

From that moment, I was no longer a PC user.

Because from that moment, I had near on zero problems. I had a big learning curve, and I disliked many of the ways the system was different, but I got used to it on the basis that stability and speed were more important to me.

If I'd stuck with my mindset that, "I <u>have</u> to use PC/Windows because that's what we use in the office", I'd still be cursing that white screen of death now.

A couple of years ago, I then exchanged my last piece of Microsoft kit for a printer, with Simon, my IT supplier/computer hero.

It was a fair deal in my opinion, he got something of value (to him) and so did I.

But... it wasn't my last piece of kit.

In fact, old habits die hard and I'd refused to change from having a Windows server.

We use it for our public drive, i.e. the drive everyone in the office can get to. All our client work is stored on it, which we then back up online.

But you know? It was frustrating.

You'd click on the network share and wait an age to connect; one of my team couldn't connect at all for some reason, and don't get me started about easy remote access.

So, I took the plunge.

I bought a NAS.

Something I should have done a long time before I did.

Sure it cost a fair few quid, but wow, do you get your value out of it... it's instant, the control panel is easy to access, reliable, and the backup systems are as easy as point and click.

What stopped me doing this years before?

The money? Nope.

The effort of moving it all? Nope.

The thought that what I had was the best because that's what I've always used? Yep.

Mindset.

That's what I'm talking about.

Mindset stops you learning.

Mindset stops you changing.

Mindset stops you making the right decisions.

So from the outset, we have to change our thinking. I have to tell you, ever since starting my business, even when listening/following a lot of seriously successful Marketers and the like, for years I struggled.

The thing is, many of these Marketers out there want to give you enough information to make a difference, because it keeps you coming back, but they don't really give you what you need to scale your business completely.

And that's because it's not easy to simply shift the way you approach your sales, marketing, and in fact, everything about your business. Changing my business for example, took more than changing my marketing.

My marketing, for the large part over the latter few years, has had a very common theme. However the approach with which I run my business, and execute my marketing, has changed dramatically. Throughout this book, you'll find other references to marketers who have seriously influenced what I do, along with how I think.

Additionally, the one thing that truly helped me grow my business was focusing on one mentor. You see, I was simultaneously in a high-end mastermind group and had a business coach and was listening to at least two other marketers for advice.

The problem with that is you get conflicting levels of importance on various aspects of your business or marketing, and the conflict ends up driving a wedge between you and the business. One of the things you've really got to have when it comes to your marketing and business, is consistency.

But the problem was, this actually ended up in the destruction of my cashflow, whereby I was so consumed with trying to follow the advice of multiple mentors I essentially 'took my eye off the ball' and brought myself to a crashing halt with no sales and no income. This in theory is easily fixed, of course, if you're able to just focus on the single most important thing: getting in sales at the right price from the right people... but we don't always have the ability to keep that single focus.

We have a business to run.

And, to top it off, being stuck in that position is simply not nice.

So to build your business you have to accept you have to learn; you almost certainly have to 'change' and, referencing my earlier point, you can't change your core personality but you probably need to instigate changes in your working life.

As a prime example of that, one of the changes I tried making in my life was to start getting up ridiculously early (5am) and work from home for a couple of hours. That extra couple of hours made a huge difference to what I could get done in a week, and in fact is one of the ways I ended up writing my first book.

Of course, it's not about making your day longer, it's about making use of your time better. So I would take a break for the kids school run, and take a long lunch to hit the gym.

Now change isn't easy, and it comes down to a few things, the primary one of course being mindset and, as I keep banging on about mindset, let's start by defining it.

Mindset is a set of assumptions, methods or notations held by one or more people, that is so established it creates a powerful incentive within this person/people that they continue or accept or adopt prior behaviours, choices, or tools.

That is to say, you believe things are the way they are because that's the way they are, and they can't be changed.

For example: *That's* the software you've got to use, *that's* the only marketing platform you can use, the *only* way to get X done is by doing ABC etc.

A classic example of this is my story about PC/Mac. Before I switched, I had used a Microsoft/Windows PC for 24 years.

But I had no choice, right? I have always used Windows and I could never use anything else.

I very much want to stress here, that it's not to say Apple are better than Microsoft - that's not my argument here, but for *me*, for what *I wanted* to do, in the way *I wanted to do it,* the Apple solution was better. My mindset for *years* prevented me from grasping it fully.

It prevented me from finding the 'Apple way' to do things, rather than just assuming it was inferior, and the 'Windows way' was better.

By accepting the mindset change, I transformed how much work I could get done, and subsequently I grew my business even faster. Something else happened too; because I got frustrated less with 'PC problems' I found my overall stress levels massively declined when it came to using the computer.

So you see, mindset is very important.

A fixed mindset will stop you achieving a lot of things; it'll stop you changing your PC, your phone, your habits, your clients, your systems.

And it's your systems that you really, almost certainly, need to change.

Sure, I don't know you, or your business. I don't know your clients. I don't know your systems.

But I know one thing: you're reading this book.

That means you want a change of some sort, right? That's most likely going to stem from the type of work you're doing, or the type of people you're doing it for, and it's all a consequence of how your marketing systems are running.

So, accept just one thing for today: something has to change.

Accept that, and you're on your way to creating the change you need to improve your business.

I'm sorry to break it to you (actually, I'm not really), but no-one cares about your business.

Apart from your significant other, your family, and perhaps close friends, no-one cares about you, your business, your logo, your brand, or pretty much anything you do.

OK, let's take an 'average' business owner (if there is such a thing) and how they might think about advertising their business or Product/Service.

The first thing you're keen to do, especially if you've been in business a few years, is make sure your logo is nice and prominent, along with "Established X Years" or similar.

The issue here is, your 'headline', whether it be on your website or your printed advertising, is often your logo. However your headline should be something to capture the reader's attention - or be directly related to the product/service they're after, or better still, be the problem that your product relates to/solves.

For example, if we're talking about offering a website, there are a whole host of problems that business owners face when it comes to sorting their online presence. Firstly, most web designers are focused on one thing: design. Secondly, many business owners don't realise the most important thing about a website is how it's marketed, not how it looks - subsequently they're not used to it generating business for them.

So you need to create a message which captures their attention by offering them something different: you need to offer them something they want.

This message must be carried throughout all of your marketing material, from everything in your brochures, to your website, your online video and even your ads. When you're speaking to potential customers you have to keep this at the forefront of your mind.

When they're first reading about your product/service, and I mean in the initial sales copy they're reading about you - your potential customers really don't care how long you've been in business, they don't need to be told about how great your product or service is, and the majority don't care about how much it costs.

There's quite a lot in that statement, so let's break it down... we have three main points to focus on here:

- They don't care how great your product/service is
- They don't care how long you've been in business
- They don't care how much it costs

You might be thinking "this is complete rubbish - of *course* they care about how good the product/service is".

Well, *yes* of course they do... but in the vast majority of cases, these are things that are considered standard. They shouldn't *have* to be told your product is good quality - especially in the initial sales copy, or that you have personal service, because these are things that you should be doing regardless and don't make you unique. When it comes to creating the desire for your product or service, you to burn these words into your mind: *What's In It For Me?*

Your readers will always be thinking it – although not consciously.

Now, a small percentage of people always buy on price, and will always look for the cheapest deal possible – but you want to *avoid* those people at all cost, because they will generally make your life hell. It's always the customers who want the cheapest deal that end up causing you the most aggravation and headaches.

The reality of the situation is, people buy based on desire, they buy something because it's going to make them feel good or solve a problem.

If all people bought on price, wouldn't everyone be driving the cheapest car?

Wouldn't *everyone* have a cheap phone instead of an iPhone?

When eating out, wouldn't *everyone* just eat at McDonalds instead of nice fancy restaurants?

And isn't it funny that when it comes to something they really want, they can 'find' the money? Perhaps that latest 50" TV just in time for the Football.

Think about smokers; they're people that *really* buy based on desire, on a regular basis. Some (a minority, obviously) have absolutely no money to speak of yet still, even when living on the edge of affordability in terms of paying their rent or keeping food on the table, will make sure they have enough tobacco to smoke.

It's plain and simple - we buy based on desire. So remember this: your brand, your logo, and everything about you is irrelevant. What's important is: what can you do for your customer that benefits them? I will put in one caveat: Brand is not that important… but *branding* is. I'll explain exactly what I mean later.

People Want To Be Sold To

Now here's a funny thing… people often think that selling is a dirty word. They think that they're no good at sales because they don't want to harass people or offer them something they don't want.

Selling is much more than simply harassing people. Yes, it's about staying in touch, but it's not about offering them something they don't want or need, it's about finding what they need, then providing them with the route to getting it. The last thing I'd ever do is 'harass' someone, but I do believe in keeping in touch with people until they buy, die, or tell you to go away.

And in fact, even the latter, sometimes you want to persist because if you have a product or service that can significantly change your prospective clients life for the better then, (and I think it was Chet Holmes who said this) it's your *moral obligation* to ensure you provide it to them.

People *want* to read about how your product/service will make their lives better.

Whether it's a more comfortable pen to write with, or the most luxurious car to drive, people *want* to be sold to. They *want* to read about how amazing it will be with this product in their life.

Once you master this process you'll find that your marketing material becomes all about how you can solve the customer's problems, and not about how you're here to help because you've been in business 25 years.

On that note, I'm not saying you should remove the fact that you've been in business 25 years either; on your website there are plenty of ways to build that in without directly injecting into the primary sales pitch. It's good to have history and even better if you've got awards or other qualifications.

These things belong primarily in the 'About Us' section of your website. That's what it's for. It's for about you, although having said that, if you write your 'About Us' content correctly, even everything that's about you can be everything about your potential customer. Just remember to focus on the problems of the reader, and how you solve them with your product/service.

Take this example: some time back, must be a few years now, I wrote up a postcard to send out to business owners. I had it critiqued by one of the biggest marketing names in the world.

My thought process behind the headline was to capture interest, essentially trying to get them to read the next line (which would promise to explain why they should read more).

The headline was:

"Do you know what Google Re-marketing is?"

(Funnily enough, almost everyone knows about Re-marketing these days - because we're all used to browsing for shoes, then getting shoes adverts everywhere… but I was doing this when Re-marketing was brand new…)

But here's the feedback I got (and it's too long ago to directly quote, but it was along these lines): Let's assume the reader doesn't know what Google Re-marketing is. The reader will almost certainly respond by saying to themselves "No, and I don't really care" as they put it in the bin.

What would be a far more suitable headline, is a headline that speaks to the *problems* of that Business Owner that Google Re-marketing fixes.

"Do You Want To Easily Reach Customers Who Visited Your Website, But Left No Details?"

Immediately you're changing the whole question. And in fact, you could go on improving that by focusing on lost profits from not reaching these people etc. The point is, you're changing the focus. It's not about a technology issue, it's about reaching potential customers who are otherwise inaccessible to you.

The sales copy can then talk about how to generate more business by reaching potential customers who have visited your website, looked at particular products/information and not purchased or enquired.

So, with all that in mind, it's time to focus on what you need to do, to make all this happen.

The thing to remember with your marketing, from your website to your PR, is that you're never finished. The vast majority of business owners I've worked with in the past, seem to treat the website as being something that "has to be done". And once it's done, that's it - it's done.

Tick it off the list and move on.

That's fine, if you just want something there for a bit of credibility, something to make you look like a 'real' business. If you want it to grow with your business however, if you want it to become a prime source of leads and/or sales... well, that takes a lot of effort.

Around mid 2013, I decided to make a change. A change in my life that would see me 'get fit'. Actually, I think I made that decision around March/April 2013, when I was watching the London Marathon on TV, but I actually took until Summer to do something about it.

You see, around 3-4 years previous to that, I'd made an active effort to get fit.

I'd got into a bit of running. I enjoyed it.

Then Josh (our first child) came along and with a combination of work and sleepless nights, the regular runs slipped to, eventually, no runs at all. Over a few years I ended up putting a bit of weight back on, so I decided enough was enough and it's time to get back into running.

Explaining this to a three year old was interesting, he couldn't figure out why I needed to. But I explained how if you don't do exercise (like him running around the house like a madman) then your tummy will get big.

I hired a Personal Trainer, with the goal of getting me running. No plans to do anything extreme, but I had to start somewhere: I could only just manage 1-2k.

I signed up for a local 10k Race, and had about 3 months to prepare, and prepare I did.

Catherine (my wife), Josh and Zach (our kids) came to cheer me on... and witnessed me absolutely in pieces at the end.

I gave it everything I had, and I was shattered.

But, having another goal was important.

When I was losing weight the first time round (before Josh) it was for the London to Southend Bike ride. I'd just got married and I wanted to really focus on changing my life for the better... but I hadn't set any subsequent goals and so I took the easy route when Josh came along: forget the training and sleep instead.

So... The first goal this time was for me to run a 10k run, but I needed a longer-term goal; both the London to Southend Bike ride and 10k run were great short-term goals.

When you hit your goals early the key is to move the goal posts. Make the goal harder.

I decided to run the London Marathon.

I wanted a guaranteed place (so I had a fixed goal) so I chose a Charity (Anthony Nolan - great charity). Again, when explaining this to Josh, he found it very confusing why I'd want to run for hours and hours, but then he got distracted by the dog chasing his tail (as kids do), so it was all good.

A few days later he said something that made me chuckle, but was also something that's a key to success. He said, "Daddy, why's your tummy still big?"

Cheeky so and so. But, and this was a point worth explaining, it's not like it disappears overnight. It's hard work, determination and discipline.

Just like with your business.

The things I'm explaining to you are not magical overnight cures. There is no magic pill that can make your business double its profits overnight.

Optimisation is the only way you can continually, consistently and organically grow your Business. Just like with the Marathon training, the changes you need to make at the start are by far the hardest.

Getting up off the sofa and getting out for a 5-10k run, on a regular basis, is hard work when you've been living your life on a sofa. And I know that all too well. Over the last year in particular, I slipped back into some really bad habits.

I'd stopped running because "I was too busy".

I'd stopped focusing on diet because "well, if I'm going to have a glass of wine the diet's out the window anyway...".

I'm sure you can piece together the rest.

So that big, long haul of marathon training I did years ago, I'm starting to go through again now. But I do it with help, not on my own. There's one book in particular, that made a big difference to my life many years ago - and I'm in the middle of re-reading at the moment to reinforce the message.

It's called "Switch: How to change things when change is hard" by Chip Heath. I can honestly say without that book, I wouldn't have implemented half the things I did in my business over the last three years (since I first discovered the book).

Not because I didn't know about them - but because it comes down to more than just knowing, you have to do something to make a difference. I highly recommend that book, although the overall ethos is carried out throughout much of what I talk about here.

In the book Switch, they reference The Happiness Hypothesis by Jonathan Haidt. Haidt talks about our emotional side as an Elephant, with the rational side as the Rider. If you just address the Rider (the rational side), you get acceptance that you should be doing something, and you know you need to do it, but the motivation is missing. You don't put your heart into it and subsequently you don't get the right results.

If you just address the Elephant (the emotional side), you get the massive desire to do something, but lack the direction and action provided by the rational side. By addressing both, you get the change you want. This really struck a chord with me, and the rest of the book, Switch, really helps reinforce how countless examples prove that if you address the Rider AND the Elephant you get results.

There's a lot more to it than that, and I couldn't do it justice here, so I heartily recommend you go and get that book once you've finished this one. It will help you when it comes to sticking with the change you need to implement.

Because that's the other thing. Sticking to it is hard.

If, like me, you're office based - your business probably revolves around you sitting at a desk a lot. I used to be primarily a Developer. That means that for nearly 10 years of my career, both employed and running my own business I spent my time at a desk, for up to 12-14 hours a day, coding.

I was sitting down, eating junk food, with minimal effort involved for tea/coffee or to get out and get more food.

But I'd end the day exhausted; OK the junk food wouldn't have helped in terms of energy levels – but even if I was eating healthily I'd end the day physically shattered.

And many people failed to understand how exhausting sitting at a desk can be.

You're using serious brain power (assuming you're working hard and have a relatively complex job...of course), and by continually focusing all day long, you're tiring out the Rider. Subsequently, the Elephant goes where it wants, not where the Rider wants it to go.

So when it came to things like dieting, the will power was absolutely devastated come night fall. Eating healthily never lasted.

The problem here is, implementing change is really hard... because when the Rider is exhausted, and you're not going in the right direction, it feels like a self-fulfilling prophecy.

If I'm honest, off the back of a bit of knowledge (that I'd had for quite some time) and the book Switch, and some serious self discipline, I started to roll out the changes I needed.

I have taken some <u>big</u> steps in the business lately, that have led to me almost entirely removing myself from the daily operations of the business. I've stopped interfering with code, and systemised the whole processes from sales to implementation.

I used to live by digging through the code we were rolling out for clients, almost line by line, picking out little issues and making it perfect.

But that's not how you grow a business.

So now - I don't have any development software on my computer. And what has that done? It allowed me to focus on what I needed to focus on.

It allowed me to write this book, for example.

It allowed me to spend more time systemising our sales processes, so that our constant stream of leads that's generated from our marketing actually convert to sales.

It allowed me to grow the business through the implementation of marketing strategies, rather than just knowing I needed to get around to doing a direct mail campaign at some point in the near future (but never getting round to it due to being too "busy")

So if I can get you to take away one message before you dig into the strategies of this book, take away this: it's a marathon, not a sprint.

Chapter Two:
Marketing Strategy

When I first started out in business, I'll be honest, I had no real idea what marketing was. I mean, I knew that it was advertising, but that was about as far as my knowledge in the subject went.

So I did what almost all business owners in this situation do: nothing. I knew I had to do *something* to generate business, so armed with nothing but the yellow pages, I started dialling out on the phone. I had a script, of sorts, and it went something like this.

"Hi, my name's Ben, and I've just started a web design company in Southend... I'm reaching out to local businesses to - more than anything - just say hi. You might not need me now, but perhaps I thought if I can just come and say hello, show my face, and if there's something I can help you with at some point that's great. Funnily enough, I'm passing your way tomorrow, around 2pm, do you have 5 minutes I can just stick my head in and drop in a brochure?"

Now to be fair, that's from memory from well over a decade (and a bit) ago... but that's close enough to the real thing (I said it enough times to remember!). Now it worked pretty well for me, in fact, in the first month of trading I generated around £10,000 (which, at the time having had a job paying me around £1,500 a month felt like a big step up).

I continued with that model for a while but I *hated* it. I dreaded the time I was due to make phone calls and over time I did it less and less, but then I found - quite obviously - I was struggling for business. So I'd hit the phones harder and it'd be alright... but I still *hated* it.

Now, remember that friend that recommended me a marketing guy? Well, it was around then that I discovered a bit more about what marketing really was. Almost overnight I felt like my whole life was about to change, and I'd now discovered the secrets that meant I was going to be rich. Rich I tell you!

We've all been sold that dream, time and again, and in fairness to this guy I was following he never promised the overnight dream specifically, but he sure as hell inferred. There are a billion other marketing 'gurus' that *will* promise overnight success. Again, I know, I've seen them (but haven't fallen for the trick).

One in particular I remember seeing a campaign for years ago, that was marketed along the lines of "copy, paste, repeat". He was selling an email sequence that was - regardless of your audience - guaranteed to make you rich.

Yeah. Right. I almost bought it just to see what it was, but I decided I'd rather keep my money. Now it's fair to say I've learnt the hard way over the years, but I'm lucky in that my 'career choice' specifically gives me an advantage.

You see, because of what I *do*, I am naturally exposed to buckets more marketing than the average business owner. Simply from consultations, I see a huge variety of marketing strategies and campaigns on a regular basis.

Then there's the clients I actually work with, so I get knee deep into what they're doing and see how it all ticks, and try and make it better. And *then* there's the stuff *I* do, and if it's one thing I do - it's test a lot of stuff on a regular basis.

Now that didn't help me say, ten years ago, because not only did I only have a handful of clients, I didn't know what marketing was, I didn't know I was selling a marketing tool, and the worst thing of all, I didn't think there was anything wrong with that.

The more I learned, and discovered, the more I realised how naive I was, and how much further I had to go before I was truly comfortable giving people 'marketing advice'. To be perfectly honest, even now, I feel like a fraud sometimes when I'm consulting with people... but the fact of the matter is, I *know* the stuff I talk about works.

This isn't some guff that I've just come up with, and it's not based on uneducated opinion. What I'm about to talk you through is years upon years of experience from directly doing this stuff, years upon years of reading books and taking courses, and years being mentored by one of Europe's finest marketing experts and copywriters.

I'd like to jump straight into some of the advanced stuff, but it's hard to do that. I remember getting really wound up at University, when I'd started my degree in Computer Networking, that almost every module started with the phrase "I'm going to start by assuming no knowledge".

I thought, "Well, what the bloody hell was the point in doing my A-Levels?!"

Now the likelihood is, that you've been running a business for a while, but for all I know you're doing no marketing, a little marketing, or so much marketing it's coming out your ears. So like my rather frustrating University lecturers, I'm going to start with the basics.

To produce anything of substance requires a level of skill, whether it's a web development project such as a complex website, or a physical development project such as a block of flats. Not only is it dependent on the people developing/creating it, but the success also comes down to a significant amount of planning and hard work.

Market, Message, Medium.

Before you even begin to build your Marketing strategy, you need to define your market. This is pretty fundamental stuff, and it's probably something you've covered a thousand and one times. But the most common factors people include when defining their market are things such as their age, location and maybe specifics to your product (i.e. if you're selling wedding rings, your market is engaged people).

But it goes much deeper than this, and I'll explain why in a second, but you need to know: Who is your ideal customer? Ask questions like:

- What do they look like?
- Where are they?
- How old are they?
- Are they Married? Single? Kids?
- How much money do they have?
- What hobbies do they have?
- What films do they like?
- What sports do they like?

These questions help build up a defined picture of your ideal customer, and that person *should* be someone that you'd like to spend time with. I make it a pretty solid rule, that I don't take on new clients that I don't *like*. If I wouldn't be prepared to go out for a pint with someone, they probably won't be a client. And in fact, I have been out with *most* of my clients at one time or another.

You might be wondering why I, a web designer at heart, am talking you through building up a picture of your ideal client in this way. Well, it's important. Because you want all your sales copy (that's the text on your website, or any sales letter/marketing material) to *talk* to that person. You want to know who you're talking to, because you want to talk to them - in your sales copy - like you would if you were 'down the pub'.

I don't mean being ridiculously informal, but if you ever receive one of my sales letters, you'll see that they're all 'conversational' and they're all just 'talking' to the person I've written to. This is very intentional.

Some people won't like the tone of voice I've used, and will chuck it in the bin.

Some people won't like the language I've used, and will chuck it in the bin.

But *some* people will.

And for every person you push away with your sales copy, you pull someone else closer. What's possibly the most important thing to take away here is, if you're writing to people you *want* to do business with because you like them - and you write in *your* voice, you'll end up with clients you *really* like and enjoy working with.

So build up the picture of your ideal customer, and then talk to them like you would in a social setting, maybe not quite so informal as to say "down the pub" - but that sort of thing. This brings us nicely to...

Now that you know who you're targeting, you need to work out what you're saying to them.

But as I've mentioned, here's the real key: by knowing exactly who you're targeting, you can talk to them in the right way. This is how you get your sales copy, or whatever it is they're reading, to appeal to them.

One fear that most have when I talk to them about this process, is that they can't afford to be picky. They can't afford to turn away business. Now that might be true, and if you're in that situation you sure as hell have to go carefully, but I chose to, before I could afford to choose to.

If I had waited until I could afford to choose who I was doing business with, I would still be waiting. Now I *did* make life a lot harder for myself, but by sacking the worst clients I had, and only working with who I *wanted* to work with, not only was I immediately happier, but everything was more profitable.

It didn't take long for things to sort themselves out, because I simply had more time to work on either up-selling the existing clients I had, or working on new clients.

But here's one little catch. You see, regardless of how similar your prospective customer might be to you, you still have to deal with the fact that *they don't know* they're similar to you. In fact, depending on what you do, they're quite possibly even sceptical about dealing with people in your industry. I know I face that problem *a lot*.

So I get around that with a very lengthy lead generation process, specifically because that allows me a lot of time to get my message across. So for example, my books act as lead magnets which bring people 'in to my world'. Then they will generally join my email list, and over a period of days, weeks, months or even years, they get to know, like and trust me enough to commit to some level of work, be it a website, marketing or perhaps just to attend an event.

Your message, i.e. what you're saying to your prospective clients, can be broken down into two categories. Your explicit message, and your implicit message.

Your Explicit Message is what you're actually writing in your sales copy. i.e. This might be text in a Newspaper Ad or a line of text in a Google Ad. This is often the thing that most people get completely wrong, and why the majority of advertisements don't pay off in the way that many others do.

And it's why they're left scratching their heads when they've developed this fancy looking full page advert in a popular magazine, but it's drawn close to zero results. The reason these adverts fail to achieve their maximum potential is because they focus on the wrong things.

To reiterate again, your prospective client doesn't care about you, your brand, your logo, your colour scheme, your ethos, your mission statement, your goals, how long you've been in business, or how many staff you have.

They care about what you can do for them. That is to say,

whatever your product or service is, it solves a problem. A problem they can't easily solve themselves. Whether it's from food and clothing to providing a recruitment service, the same rule applies.

You make their life easier or better. One of the two.

So your message needs to make that obvious... blatantly obvious. You need to practically spell it out, first with a very clear headline, and then with compelling, engaging copy. I'll come to that a bit later, but it's easily summarised by simply saying - focus on the benefits and the *result* of what you're offering.

Then we have your *implicit message,* and it's as obvious as it sounds - it's what's implied by what you say. For example by saying:

"We only work with a relatively small number of clients at any one time one on one, helping them to grow their business. Our premium web design and marketing services are engineered specifically to help high performing businesses perform even higher. With a strong track record, our portfolio of case studies prove that our strategies consistently deliver results."

The explicit message is obvious enough, it's what I've said... but the implication is that first of all, we offer a premium service, and as such the price associated with our services is likely to be relatively high. I don't mean extortionate, I simply mean... premium.

This seriously affects your positioning.

For example, it's unlikely you'd read that statement, then expect us to do a website for £500. Or frankly even £2000... And you really do want to position yourself at the top. Not only is it just *easier* to work with people at this level, but it's far more profitable and enjoyable too.

Of course the service has to reflect the price - I don't mean position yourself at the top if you're selling cheap tat or delivering a poor service (you won't last long, if you do that). Whether you're selling a unique product/service or a product/service that a million other people sell, you can still position yourself at the top with your message.

The final question in the mix here, is *where* do you put your message? Social media? Email? Newspapers? Your website? Radio? TV?

The thing is many people I know are always looking for the best medium to use, especially if it's "cheap" to advertise in/on, without much concern as to whether their market (i.e. who you're talking to) or message (i.e. what you're saying) is right.

They'll fit the message to the medium they want to use and hope their market reads it. For example, by posting to Facebook over and over, regardless of whether they actually get results from it. There are cases where organically posting to Facebook can be a good idea, but as a rule of thumb it's not something you should really be focusing on. It's an enormous drain on your time and energy for little to no reward. You're essentially trying to shoehorn your message to the wrong medium, or in other words, you're using the wrong tool for the job.

That reminds me of a time when I was younger. I grew up in the 80's so actually going by today's standards it's a miracle I'm alive apparently, but anyway... This story begins when I was around 14 or so. I'd arranged to go on a bike ride with a friend, but I had a problem. My bike wasn't fast enough (I think it had a problem with the gears or something, I really can't remember the specifics).

But I do remember, the bike not being fast enough was a serious problem for a young teenager. So, I arranged to cycle to a friends house, borrow his bike, then ride on to meet this other friend. To be fair, his bike was pretty awesome - it was damned fast and finely tuned, but there was one problem.

Actually, one quite, major problem, in the grand scheme of things.

The brakes didn't work properly.

Well, this led to some amusing collisions whilst out on the ride with my friend, but hey - it was a great laugh. Once the fun was over, I decided to head home. I was cycling down down one of the main roads in my home town, which had a police station on it.

Now, if you're cycling along the pavement (which I was, I think it was pre-cycle path and the roads were too busy), you cross two roads. The first was all clear so I kept going at speed.

I thought, "I'm not far from my friends house (that I'm returning the bike to) now, so let's make the most of it on this stretch."

It was great, up to the point I saw a police car coming out the station, stopped right where I needed to cross. I had a decision to make. Crash into the police car at full speed, or try and skid the bike over and land on my feet somehow.

I figured, if I turned the front wheel whilst trying to brake as hard as possible with my back, I might just be able to pull this off and look really cool.

Man, I did *not* look cool.

Full on collision with a lamp post.

Over the handlebars, and into the post.

I collapsed on the ground, seriously winded and with serious pain all over but the biggest injury was my pride. I had no choice but to stand up and cough "yep, no I'm fine thanks" to the lady and her daughter that had come up to check if I was ok.

I got back on the bike and took a very sheepish ride back to my friends house, apologised for scratching the hell out of his bike, and rode mine home.

I was lucky that I had only fractured my fingers, which I didn't find out about until about 4 hours later when my mum got home and saw my fingers had turned a kind of blue-black and rushed me to A&E.

Oops.

But my point here is, that if you're not using the right tools, or the equipment you're using isn't up to standard, you're at risk of looking a bit of a muppet, along with getting seriously winded. Or worse.

And if you're using Facebook to regularly post updates, and you rely on that as a source of business, then you're effectively riding a bike with no brakes. Because whatever Facebook decide to do to the way your posts are displayed to your fan-base, is their decision, and theirs alone. You cannot control it, nor can you have any impact on it. But it can have a big impact on you.

Consider all the people that complained when Facebook really started tweaking their "algorithm", which works out what content to display to people based on what they (Facebook) thought the reader wanted to see. Facebook have made countless revisions to their algorithm over the years and will continue to do so. Why? I'll cover more in the 'Getting Found' section of this book, but for the minute, just trust me on this.

The opposite is true of course, for those of you that harness the Ads system within Facebook to make sure you're targeting the right Market - and you're always going to be delivering the Message because, well, you're paying for it.

I mention Facebook, because it's a good medium to use. It's useful for almost every business, from Fish & Chips to Accounting. Their ability to laser target prospects has got really good over the last year or two… but we're focused very much online here.

When it comes to more physical mediums, such as newspapers

or magazines, choosing the right one can be tricky. You need to be in control of which Medium you choose, rather than the other way around.

Find your Message, define your Market, then find your Medium to deliver that message to your Market. It's a simple concept, and I think deep down many business owners know it, but they forget or get caught up in special offers for advertising in certain places etc.

Direct Response vs Brand Marketing

There are two types of marketing, Brand Marketing and Direct Response Marketing. One of the easiest mistakes to make when starting an advertising campaign is to think it's a good idea to do it for "brand awareness". Unfortunately, unless you have *very* deep pockets, a brand marketing campaign is not going to be the best use of your cash.

A multinational, multi-million pound company is quite capable of developing a series of brand awareness adverts which use advanced techniques to drive up sales... They're able to spend £25 Million with a combination of TV Ads, Billboards, Paper Adverts and Mailshots. Now, if you've got a product for consumers, and a spare £25 Million - go for it (but given that you're reading this book, I'd be quite surprised).

So that's not going to work for your average small business, so we have to be smarter. What's even worse, is that most small business owners end up brand advertising, without even realising it. Partly because they're probably influenced by 'what everyone else does' and partly because they're proud of their brand/logo and want everyone to see it.

The thing is, it really doesn't work well at all, when it comes to advertising in a newspaper, magazine or online, but the added benefit of doing a carefully implemented direct response advertising campaign is, that if done properly it can work as brand awareness as well.

Put simply, direct response marketing is a measurable form of advertising that is proven to be highly effective. You need a call to action, and it should be a convincing, irresistible offer to the reader, which conveys to them not only why to contact you (or provide you with their contact details) but how.

Brand advertising simply wastes money for the average small business owner.

So what we *want* to focus on, is direct response marketing. Specifically, you want to focus on generating leads through your marketing activities. Let's take a very simplistic example. Let's say that Bob, is looking for a new TV, and let's say that you sell TVs.

It's an extremely crowded market place, and you don't make much margin compared to 'the big boys'. So how could you *possibly* make your marketing work?

The easy answer is, stop advertising for the sale.

One of the easiest, and quickest ways to go out of business, is to try and compete on price. When you're selling TVs, in a crowded market place, you might suggest there's no way you could do anything else.

But here's the trick: People who buy new TVs rarely go to the local electrical store and say "cheapest TV please".

I mean, they *might*, don't get me wrong... but it's *rare*.

It's a relatively small purchase in the grand scheme of things, compared to say, houses, cars, and holidays... but it's still quite a big purchase. More importantly, for many of 'the masses', it's probably something they'll end up sitting in front of for nearly 25% of their life. They want to make sure they "get a good one".

When I bought my last TV, I spent days researching.

One of the things I would have been a sucker for, would be some sort of up to date guide on choosing the right TV. Something that gives you information you can relate to, rather than dozens of technical specifications that most people have no clue about what they mean.

It's really important to use Google to get found, but the problem is, when you're selling something as popular and potentially expensive as a TV, you need to maximise your return on investment.

So if you have some expert knowledge to impart, and an in depth knowledge of all your products on offer, you can provide that information in the form of a guide. And, if you swap that information for someone's details, you can then (with their permission) send them additional follow up material. This is referred to as a 'lead magnet', and typically someone signs up for your lead magnet, and then gets your regular email marketing.

This should really be one of the primary calls to action on your website… someone can simply pop in their name and email, and you email them a copy of your guide. Nice and simple.

If you're not able to track the effectiveness of an advert that's running, change it. You *must* be able to test and measure anything you do (this applies to everything, not just advertising).

Not so long ago I was chatting to a competitor of mine, and we got on to the subject of tracking. He was adamant that his responsibility ended when he'd generated a click. Sadly, I don't think he's alone in that opinion and that makes for a whole industry of marketing agencies that are purely focused on driving 'traffic'.

I don't really care how many clicks we generate, per se, I'm much, *much* more interested in how many *leads* those clicks have generated. Specifically, I'm interested in what ads, what audiences, and what landing pages have generated those leads (a landing page is literally just the page where someone 'lands' when they've clicked on an advert).

Of course not all leads are generated online, so you can stay on top of your tracking by simply asking how/where they found out about you. Some of the advanced online ways of tracking include automatically tagging a contact in your management software based on which advert they clicked on.

I'm deliberately glossing over many of these terms because I'll come to them in so much more detail in a bit, but what I'm trying to convey here is: Tracking is essential.

It's the like age old, semi-comedic and semi-depressing phrase which goes: "I know 50% of my marketing works, and 50% is a waste of money. I just don't know which 50% works."

But you don't have to be a rocket scientist to start tracking; and it's invaluable in the long term. You can track anything - whether it's a Google Ad, or a postcard… everything can be tracked.

For example, you could send out a batch of postcards to a certain area with a particular offer, whether it be a free guide or discount code – it doesn't matter - you either send them to a tracked page on your website so you can measure the success or you get them to call you with a particular code to claim their special offer.

Which is better?

I can't answer that, you have to test and measure (you'll get sick of me saying that) to get the results. Anyone who tells you one is better than the other, is wrong for doing so. They're wrong, not because one is better than the other, but because it just *depends*.

It depends on your market, it depends on your message and your medium, but more importantly it just plain depends on everything you're doing.

The paper you advertised in, the quality of the card you used on your postcards, the font you used in your advert, the size of the headline in the sales letter, the size of the phone number in the call to action... the list is endless.

Opt-In Marketing

So I've mentioned lead magnets briefly; this is where we're creating a guide to offer in exchange for their details. Look at your website right now. Is there a compelling offer? Is there a reason for someone to give you their details?

I hate to tell you, but 'request a quote' doesn't count.

Neither does a free newsletter.

Don't get me wrong - you'll get some signups from a newsletter, but really, who *cares* about a newsletter? What's in it? *Why* should they give you their contact details just to get 'news' about your company? How's that of interest or relevance to them? Specifically, how's that a *benefit* to them?

You can't expect the reader to have any interest in your company, and even if you've got a lead magnet on offer - you can't expect them to just take your word for it that the guide you're providing is great.

You still have to sell something that's free because actually... it's not free. You're asking for personal information. You're asking for their contact details.

So ask yourself this, when you look at your page offering a download in exchange for their details: What's the benefit? What's in it for them?

To spell it out - simply saying you're the best in your field or you're a dedicated team is irrelevant, but by selling the benefits of the outcome of what you provide, not the service/widget itself, you'll generate more business than ever.

This is critical within all your marketing.

It applies to *everything* you do.

When writing your sales copy, you need to focus on what you do specifically, that really benefits the customer - and more importantly why they can't get that anywhere else. With what I do for example, there are thousands upon thousands of web designers/marketing 'agencies' out there. Trying to compete with them on price is stupid.

The problem with my competition, is that any Joe Bloggs off the street can set up a business and say they do marketing. What they *mean* is they'll do your website and maybe Google Ads or SEO or something. There's no barriers, no regulations, no qualifications required.

So when it comes to working out your message, you need to have in the front of your mind your Unique Selling Point (USP).

How can you make a difference to their life?

For example, rather than "Number one store in town for Sofa Covers" – you could say "Make your Sofa look brand new again for a fraction of the cost".

The difference? You're selling the benefit, the product is the way they get the benefit. The customer gets a brand new sofa look, but they've maybe only spent £300 rather than £3000. That's a pretty attractive offer for anyone.

With this style of marketing, you may have guessed, we're not looking for an immediate sale. You clearly have to make it *possible* for people to 'jump the queue' and buy whatever you're selling immediately - but mostly, we're just looking to let people give us permission to give them information, and permission to sell to them. This is 'opt in' or 'permission' marketing.

That is to say, the people that give you their details (the leads) effectively do so with the explicit permission that you can send them additional information and subsequently 'sell to them'.

You don't want to immediately 'harass' people, and inundate them with sales material, because they'll just get bored. We're genuinely looking to try and help people here, we're genuinely looking to give people useful information.

By doing so, you massively increase your positioning as an expert and trusted authority, and so in time, become the *only* logical choice, rather than competitor X down the road.

That is how I build my USP.

We build a relationship so that the prospective client knows, likes and trusts us... and when it comes to choosing a web designer, naturally we're the only choice. A specific case of this comes to mind.

Someone had been on my list for a long time, perhaps a year or more.

I'd never spoken to him, but he'd clicked to say he was interested in one of my events.

This meant, when I was pulling off a certain report, he was included in a round of phone calls for a special offer for the event.

He came to the event... and we enjoyed a few (...quite a few) beers together. We got to know each other better.

Then some time later, I was running a particular offer for web design.

Again, some interest was shown, a follow up phone call later, and money was transferred within 24 hours.

I have countless examples of this, and it's proof enough to me that this marketing model *works*. But it takes time, and it takes effort.

Of course, I know people that do this with just a fraction of the effort they should, and don't get the results. It's a huge mistake to take people's personal details in exchange for a guide or similar, where they're then clearly expressing an interest in your product/service/widget, and to then do nothing with them.

What's Your Marketing Budget?

This is a question I used to ask a lot.

I was stupid.

I admit that.

I did it for a reason: I did it because I had been 'trained' to go for the sale as soon as possible. So by finding out what their budget was and by coming in under budget, I could be sure of an easier sale than if I was coming in way over budget.

This is a remarkably common strategy, but it's enormously stupid.

Firstly, because it let them be in control of my pricing. That's just ridiculous. The more I think about it now the more I want to travel back in time and give myself a huge slap. The prices I charge reflect the time, energy and skills that go into delivering the end result. What *your* budget is compared to that, is irrelevant. It sounds really harsh to say so, but if you can't afford our fees, that's unfortunate, but it's not my problem.

It's one of the reasons I wrote books, and guides, and produce other content, and run events... because I *do* want to help everyone - but I can't help everyone one on one.

By cutting my prices in the past, I've caused myself cashflow issues time and time again, because I've not just cut my prices - I've also massively cut my profits - just to appease someone else's marketing budget.

The thing is, if you're offered a discount, you'd be mad not to accept it. I used to cut my price over, and over, and over again just to get a sale. People *don't* buy on price, but if you're ready to buy and then someone says "Oh and it's now 20% cheaper" why would you say no?!

It reminds me of when I was shopping at a sunglasses shop, which is shut down now (surprise surprise). I'd taken our chosen sunglasses to the checkout. I'll point out, in case it's not obvious, I knew exactly how much these sunglasses were going to cost.

They had price tags.

That's the point of price tags, right?

I literally had my credit card by the terminal, ready to shove in and let them take my money... when she said "Let me just see what discounts I can do for you..."

Wait, what?!

I mean, I wasn't going to complain *obviously*, and she reduced the price by something crazy like 20%. What was I going to say? "Oh no, please charge me full price pretty please...", no... Instead, I just shrugged, said "Cool", and paid.

I see this time and again, with people terrified to charge the right price. I can say that with confidence because I'm talking from first hand experience... I have been in that situation many, many times. Sat in a room, talking through everything you're going to do in great depth, and then after about an hour or two of talking, getting to the price.

And then the fear sets in.

"Am I charging too much?"

"Maybe I should reduce it."

"Maybe I should say I'm going to give them a discount."

"Maybe I should ask them how much *they* want to pay..."

It's all counter productive of course. If you've established a price for your services, that's the price you should charge, because anything *less* than that, and you're underselling yourself. You're cutting your profits and that's *bad* for your business *which means* it's bad for your client - because if your business suffers, your service to your client suffers.

Secondly (returning to "Why it's stupid to have a marketing budget"), it's stupid because no-one should *have* a Marketing budget. I don't mean by that, you should just spend every penny you have on marketing, because that'll ruin your cashflow (well, probably).

But the idea of a *fixed* budget, picked arbitrarily and stuck to, means you're specifically limiting your potential income. Your budget should be carefully calculated per acquisition. i.e. What are you prepared to spend to get a customer?

As a general rule (and it will vary from business to business) what you're prepared to spend to get a client shouldn't be justified by what they're going to spend with you just once. It should be determined by what they're going to spend with you over time, *or* based on the potential referrals they will pass to you. I have yet to see a business that has no room for repeat business AND no room for referrals.

Those two factors should be a strong consideration in your overall lifetime value of a client. For me, I do value the referrals, and I get them a lot, but for simplicity I don't incorporate that into my calculation on what I'm prepared to spend to get someone.

For the sake of argument, I'll make up some figures here. Let's say an average client is worth over a three year period, £50,000. But a *great* client, is worth up to £250,000 or more. Determining who's average and great, is difficult until they've been running for a while, maybe even as long as a year.

With those sort of client values, you can see why you can then spend literally £1,000's to get a client on board.

"But, I only sell gadgets for £1.99, how can I *possibly* compare to those sort of figures?", I hear you cry. Well, even if you *do* sell £1.99 gadgets, you can work out what that customer is worth to you over three years. Factor in perhaps the odd referral, assuming you implement (which you should) a good referral strategy.

The point is not the scale of the numbers, the point is knowing the numbers in the first place. So with this in mind, factoring in referrals and repeat business - you might be able to run with a budget of £5 or even £10 to get a customer.

So whilst you have to watch cashflow, obviously, you could be driving your competitors *nuts* because you're spending 5x the initial sale to get a customer on board. But you *know* it'll pay off because they'll have paid you back within 12 months and in years 2 and 3 you're generating profit from that customer way beyond your competitors wildest dreams.

Getting The Opt-In

If you're an e-commerce website, you'll measure your success based on the number of sales you get, versus the number of visitors you get. If you're operating a 'traditional' lead generating site, i.e. instead of going for sales, we're looking to get enquiries, you look at the number of enquiries vs the number of visitors.

Either way, this gives you a conversion rate. An e-commerce website typically has a conversion rate of anything around 0.5% to 2%. That means, if you have 1000 people visit, you might get between 5 and 20 sales.

If you've got a more typical 'lead generating' site, which just has a call back option or similar, you might get something like 5% conversion rate. These figures are plucked out of the air, by the way, just to help me demonstrate my example.

But in real terms, that means for every 100 people that come to your site, 95 aren't interested, or at least, they *appear* to not be interested.

So the question is, how do you get these figures up?

I alluded to this somewhat earlier. I discussed that most people go for the sale, but you should offer a lead magnet instead. A guide, of some sort.

The whole purpose of your website is not to generate you sales per se (unless you're e-commerce in which case *clearly* it should) but it should generate you leads. Although I will say, even if you're e-commerce, your site should still be generating you leads as well as sales.

The critical questions are:

1. How do we do that?

and

2. What do we do with the leads once we've got them?

Before I delve too much into *that* (the 'follow up'), this approach takes adjustment., and I completely and utterly understand the resistance in changing your approach. So the question is, why should you do 'lead generation' over 'traditional marketing'?

I don't mean traditional marketing like offline marketing, such as direct mail and newspapers (although Direct Mail is damn important part to any good marketing strategy) I mean marketing in the way that most business owners would go about.

Even the pretty savvy ones who realise it's about 'direct response' would still place an advert in the paper, or even on Google Ads, advertising their product or service. Most would probably be promoting their brand, but even if the Ad was very 'direct response' orientated, it would still be just promoting a product or service.

Lead Generation takes a different approach.

It's a longer approach, and it won't likely return you *quick* profits (ordinarily, although sometimes you get a nice surprise) but in the long term it will generate you *more* profits.

As a fair disclaimer, sometimes it can take a long time to realise that the type of leads you've generated aren't 'right', so you need to change your lead generation strategy. By 'right' I simply mean, they're the wrong people for your list. This can come down to inaccurate targeting, the wrong copy / adverts, or just a bit of bad luck. Sometimes, you need to 'write off' your current investment – and that can be a bitter pill to swallow.

But the great thing is, that money is never *wasted* (unless you've done something stupid, of course) because you've learnt whether something does or doesn't work. I tell you this for no other reason than many other 'experts' and 'gurus' out there won't reveal to you (amongst their shiny promises) that you can invest £1,000's into leads which despite your best efforts, are the wrong target market. They don't generate you business and you've lost your investment.

I've been in that position.

I've suffered from that.

And I tell you this because no-one ever told me.

I've varied between having nothing but pure lead magnet driven websites (as a primary business website) and a straight forward "get a quote now" type call to action. I've found best results from a healthy mix of both.

But I struggled, at first.

It was my fault, of course, for not taking a careful and considered approach to implementing this type of business model. I'm not blaming the people that gave me the information in any way, shape or form... but I do think it's fair to say, you need to implement these changes *gradually*. Unless you're adamant you're getting *nothing* from your website or marketing of course, in which case - go nuts.

But if your website and/or marketing is working to a reasonable standard - then know this: If you stopped all your current marketing, and moved to Lead Generation overnight – you could quite possibly do yourself a lot of harm.

That's fine if you've got the cash reserves to ride it out (and it *will* pay you enormous dividends in the long run) but if you're 'tight' on cash flow, be very careful with what you do.

I'll talk more about this in a bit, but you can phase things in. You can start by running simultaneous adverts/campaigns which go to specific 'lead generation only' landing pages, and you can just add some extra lead magnets to your main website to start driving up leads.

Implemented correctly this form of business model is both enjoyable and profitable. I've enjoyed having people come into my world as a 'lead' and subsequently I have been writing daily emails for (at time of writing) over six years now. I've always enjoyed it (despite it not being profitable in the early days).

And in spite of my warning, I'm adamant that every business should be working this way. My point, and my warning, is to ensure you adjust to this model smoothly. Unlike I've done in the past where I've thrown all caution to the wind and gone in head first without thinking of the consequences of it not working.

So getting the right sort of leads comes down to a few things, but most importantly you can't rely on just one form of communication to win you the business. Whether that's a product sale or service you're offering, you must speak to people via different mediums in a way that is appropriate for that medium.

That is to say, you wouldn't want to write a daily email via Twitter... but you might want to write a blog with a call to action, and then post that via Twitter.

Then you have Re-marketing.

Re-marketing is where you advertise to people that have been to your website/landing pages, but haven't given you their details.

We've all seen this happen.

Browsing for shoes, then suddenly you see nothing but adverts for shoes. Re-marketing is important for lead generation, because if people don't take action on the landing page the first time, it doesn't mean they're not interested.

I do this all the time, where I'll look at something and I'm on the verge of putting in my details – and something happens. Perhaps I'm called up by a client, perhaps the kids have distracted me, perhaps the doorbell went. Whatever it is, I've closed the page and forgotten about it.

I've got into a habit of 'saving things' on Facebook – I can't remember what it's called but you can basically add pages/adverts into a list of saved things. This is useful because again, most of the time I'm looking at Facebook I'm on the go – so if my train arrives or I get to where I'm going – I'll close it and forget about it. But then, I don't know the last time I looked at my saved items, so it's with good intention I save it, but it's still useless. Re-marketing helps pick up those people that *are* interested, but have just been distracted.

Once you've got the 'opt in', the question is, what do you do with the 'lead'. I use email marketing as the primary form of communication, simply because although sending 100's or 1000's of letters every day would probably bring me the same result, the logistical headache doesn't bear thinking about.

Plus, and actually probably more to the point, you'd have to have a fair amount of cash flow to sustain it long enough to get the profits from it. So email is awesome, because it's easy and next to free when compared against other forms of communication.

However on its own it's not nearly as effective as when *combined* with direct mail. Direct mail has a 'bad press' because it's deemed as expensive, and people don't want it. Well, I totally disagree. I think people do like stuff through the post.

You know, personalised stuff.

Most people only send out bills or similar through the post, so to have something personalised and possibly even entertaining or informative helps you stand out. Since making Direct Mail a key part of my marketing and follow up, my results have significantly increased, and it's fair to say the same applies to my clients.

So to summarise very quickly before I get on with the subject at hand: Lead generation works, but take care not to jump in with both feet without realising first, you may take a dip in income whilst the lead generation builds. Most importantly – targeting the right leads is *critical* because it can take weeks and months for you to realise that the leads you have are totally inappropriate for you. The best approach to take is to introduce strategies slowly, and surely.

Something that's important to know is, more and more people are recognising that lead generation works better than going 'straight for the sale'. Still not many, in terms of the overall number of businesses, but every day more and more people are getting more educated in the realms of opt-in marketing.

You're getting more and more educated.

So the longer you wait to get started on this, the more people there will be trying to run the same 'offer' in exchange for an email or name, and in return the person subscribing gets a bucket load of emails too.

But let's back up a bit … I'm getting a bit ahead of myself.

Let's just re-explain the whole scenario of lead generation so that there's no confusion, and let's talk about exactly how we're going to go about it. Lead generation is the process by which you ask the person visiting your site to give you their details, in exchange for some sort of offer. This might be a free report, a PDF download, a book or a guide, it might be videos or it might be a course.

Whatever the offer, the lead gives you their name, email and maybe phone or even physical address. You then give them your report, book, whatever. Then, and most importantly here, you need to follow up.

It's this latter part that most people get substantially wrong. As someone who does a lot of lead generation, I'm dismayed when I see people getting full contact details from their leads, and not doing anything more than just emailing them. If you've got their physical address, and your potential value of that client is worth it, why the hell not send them regular lumpy mail?

Lumpy mail, being mail which is lumpy (it's pretty self explanatory). I'll often send out things from plant pots, to chocolate bars, torches/flashlights, Rubik's cubes, chocolate coins.... The list is endless. It stands out far more than regular mail, and builds curiosity which in turn, gets your mail opened. After all, if you've got a shiny envelope on your desk with a lump in it – and you're not expecting anything, you're not just going to leave it sitting there, are you?!

Whatever the process or system of your follow up, you *must* follow up. And, in the initial follow ups, I'd have a strong call to action for if they're interested in buying your product or service immediately – that way you're going to capture the 'hot' leads better.

The idea of lead generation is that you have a period of time where you're getting to know your leads better (or, more accurately, they're getting to know you). This is where you want something like an automated sequence of emails to go out over time, perhaps days, weeks or even months.

Sure you can put a call to action in, in case anyone wants to buy there and then, but I would keep offers constrained to certain timeframes.

Time constrained offers tend to yield better results.

The way I run my sequence, on a simplistic level at least, is to run a series of around 30 emails before selling. There's then a 3 or 4 day selling period, with a break, then a subsequent selling period selling a different product.

They then fall over onto my daily emails, whereby I send daily broadcast emails to my list. I then alternate offers over time, and talk about different products/services and subsequently get sales from different leads and different times.

This is ultimately because most people are not ready to buy. Just because you're ready to sell, and you've got a fantastic offer – doesn't mean your lead will have any interest in actually buying. There are gazillions of reasons why people don't buy, so you just need to follow up until they buy, die or tell you to go away.

(They tell you to go away with email marketing by unsubscribing).

But I would 100% mix follow up with using direct mail too.

Of course, with lead generation you've got a lot of different sources of leads from both online and offline. Before I delve into each platform/source, and explain the differences in strategy for each, let's talk a little more about 'how' online lead generation works.

You need to have worked out your sales funnel, which essentially means you need to know what you're doing with the leads once you've got them. One of the worst things you can do, is what I've done in the past – where you accumulate some leads but then do bugger all with them. Then you wonder why online lead generation doesn't work.

Sorting out your sales funnel is actually easier than it sounds in many respects. Sure, you've got to put some time and effort into it, I'd be lying if I said it'd be quick and easy, but it's not that complicated.

You need to sign up to someone like Mailchimp, AWeber, Keap (formally Infusionsoft), Ontraport, ClickFunnels, etc. the list is endless. Technology changes regularly, there are new suppliers all the time, so I'm not going to 'commit' myself to recommend one particular supplier.

Either way, sign up with someone and get a series of emails set up in a sequence (you can usually use the platforms help/support to get you going initially). You don't need a vast amount of emails to get you off the ground - but you would need at least seven or eight, I'd say.

Then you need to work out what your lead magnet will be. This will be what you're offering to the person who's landed on your page in exchange for their contact details. Once you've got a lead magnet in place (and I will talk about this in more depth in a little while) for the moment just imagine something like a 2-3 page A4 PDF document, which contains useful information on the subject revolving around your product/service.

Once you've got a lead magnet ready to go, you need a landing page. Now here's where it can get a little complicated but – fortunately – there are tools to make it easier. Again there are so many platforms out there I won't recommend a particular one, but if you head over to dbobible.co.uk and click on resources, there's some recommendations inside the resources area.

With almost all of them though, you can knock yourself up a landing page in a matter of minutes, though realistically, you're probably going to spend a good few hours on it and maybe longer. Once you've done it a few times you'll start to get quicker and quicker at it.

The great thing about offering a guide, though, is it's like I've said before – you're changing the game. You're not putting together a landing page to promote your business anymore, you're putting together a landing page to promote your guide/report/whatever.

Your guide/report/whatever then promotes you, either directly or indirectly. That call to action on the landing page should always be to fill out their details. Now, as a general guide, the more details you ask for, the lower the response rate. Not *always* the case and that's why you need to test it, but also (and this is a total generalisation) the more details you get the higher quality the lead.

So it's swings and roundabouts. 100 names/email leads could be as strong as just 5 full name/address/phone number leads.

Once you've got the lead come in, they should be automatically followed up by your autoresponder and in the long run - as long as the copy in your emails is good, you have additional follow up as well (ideally some direct mail, maybe some telesales too) and you have good strong call to actions with good offers and reasons to respond, etc, you *should* get good conversion rates over time.

If you don't, you might want to consider looking at your source of leads, whether it be the targeting (the market) or the medium you're using. If you're convinced your targeting is right, then you need to look at your offer. If you're talking to the right audience, but they aren't converting into clients, then the likelihood is - what you're offering isn't what they want.

Talking of your targeting, *where* do you actually get your leads from? You have a multitude of sources for potential customers, and this is where you must start by focusing on the three M's that I covered before - Market, Message, Medium.

When you've found a way to target just your Market, deliver the right Message on the right Medium. I'll focus on more of this as we get deeper into the book, but a typical example is that you run an Ad on Google which is triggered by a certain keyword/phrase. Perhaps someone is looking for an estate agent.

You run an Ad, along the lines of "Thinking of selling? read this first". They're then taken to a page which lists the benefits of your free guide on choosing an estate agent, and how to avoid the common pitfalls such as X, Y and Z.

In exchange for this valuable guide, all you want in return is their name and email and the opportunity to send them more information.

Over time, you send them regular emails. They might not read your emails every day, or even open all of them, but over time they become accustomed to your name. When they choose to buy /sell, the chances are greatly enhanced that they will choose you, rather than returning to Google.

It's also a good way to weed out those that you don't want to do Business with. The types of people you'll have a personality clash with, for example. Every now and then I'll get an unsubscribe that makes me chuckle - because they'll leave a complaint on their way out. It reminds me that what I'm doing works, because either this person would never have bought from me, or they'd have been a nightmare of a client when they did.

The thing is, you can use this to your advantage, and use it as fuel for one of your other daily emails. Take this quote from one of my Daily Emails:

"...but I do just take a little notice (only a little, mind) when someone 'complains' as they unsubscribe. Mainly because I want to watch my complain rates and ensure I don't get slapped by my email provider.

I had to chuckle when I read this comment.... this was from a lady called Di. She took my book from me at an exhibition a while ago, and I explained I would email out daily. You'd have thought that after the first few emails she'd unsubscribe if it was "unexpected". This was weeks ago now.

Anyway, the comment she left as she marked my emails as "unsolicited SPAM" and remarked it was: "an opinionated daily rant".

Well, she got one thing right: daily."

The thing is, yes, my emails are opinionated, they are emails that relate to my opinion and to my outlook on both marketing and life. But this is entirely intentional… beyond that in fact, it's entirely the *point* of daily emails.

They're also, generally speaking, entertaining, but an important point to raise here is, that whilst I get a lot of opt-ins, opens, clicks and unsubscribes, that's not what email marketing is all about. Nope. It's not about open rates, or click rates, or anything like that, despite what all the other marketers will tell you.

It's about one thing. How much business have you had as a result of your email marketing? Sales. Cash in the door.

I don't particularly care if I get 1 unsubscribe or 100 unsubscribes a week because I offend everyone with my opinion. I don't really care if I get a 56% open rate and 15% click through rate. These can be indicators for sure, but they're nothing to obsess over. I've used these to make me aware of an issue; for example, when the open rate was a mere 10% of its usual figure, I realised something was up - and indeed there was a technical issue. The primary thing I really care about - is whether I'm getting the sales or not.

Forming The Strategy

So far, I've covered a lot of the basics. I've covered the

essentials that let you start building a proper marketing strategy, something you can work with over time. What I'll talk through now is, step by step, everything I'd consider when consulting with a client and building their marketing strategy. But first, let's define the difference between strategy and tactics, because most people confuse the two (I did, for a long time).

Your *strategy* is to attract leads, and follow up with them, until they buy from you. Then, once they've bought from you, you follow up more, until they buy from you again or give you a referral (depending on your business, it may be repeat-purchase or it might be one offs.... Even in most cases where people think it's one offs, people still repeat, they just don't repeat with the same person, so this is really valuable).

Your *tactics* are to use things like Google Ads, Email Marketing, Direct Mail, etc... they're the individual parts of the overall puzzle that make your whole strategy work.

Take daily emails.

I send out daily, but as I've mentioned before, I'd probably get the same results if I sent say, a postcard daily. Or a letter. The point is, email is the tactic that's easiest to implement, to achieve what I want to achieve: constant follow up.

Your business requires a constant flow of sales. What your numbers are depends on you, your business, your product/service, and how much money you want to make.

If, for example, it takes you 10 hours to service one client, and you work 40 hour weeks, your maximum capacity is 4 clients per week (with no room for a breaks...!).

If however, you sell widgets for £500 and it takes 10 minutes to produce/package and send them out, the maximum you can send is 6 per hour, so working over 8 hour days and with 5 day weeks, that's a maximum of 240 new customers a week.

You'll find it easier to sell to your existing customers, so if you were selling the widgets, you could try and sell to your existing customer base by way of encouraging referrals or repeat sales. So rather than purely attracting new customers, and needing 240 new customers a week, you manage to sell 60 to your existing customer base, so you'd actually only need 180 new customers that week. And as your customer base grows, so does the number of repeat customers and referrals.

So, how do we attract new customers to your business? We've talked about identifying your target market and building up a persona of your ideal customer. Defining their characteristics, their interests etc... that's important, but the next step is identify the burning problem that those people have. It doesn't matter if you sell fish and chips, houses, or kettles... whatever your product offers, it solves a problem.

Identifying that problem is absolutely crucial to creating your strategy, whether you're solving their hunger problem, not having enough space at home (or even, not having a home of their own), or simply just being able to make a *perfect* cup of tea with the right kettle.

You cannot have a robust strategy without that problem clear in your mind.

But it goes deeper than that, because once you've identified the problem, that's only half the battle. You then need to create a list of reasons WHY your product/service is the best solution. Put yourself in their shoes, then consider: *What's In It For Me?*

You've got to focus on all the true benefits of your product that alleviate the burning need of your prospect. Are they hungry? Want a bigger house? Waste less time waiting for the kettle to boil or want zero limescale or whatever. The point is, your strategy hinges on these two questions:

- What's your prospect's burning problem?

- How are you the solution?

I strongly recommend grabbing yourself a notepad and starting to jot down some of these ideas. Together, throughout the rest of this section of the book, we'll get all the bits you need for your marketing strategy.

Once you've got that sorted, you then need to identify the type of person you want to work with. Because, for example, what I offer is technically suitable and will help millions of business owners all over the World. But I don't want to help everyone.

Because:

- I don't have the capacity to help millions of people one on one
- I want to charge a significant premium to work with me

My best types of client, are those that understand marketing to a good level, run successful businesses, have a desire to grow, and have the guts to actually do what's required. Many clients I've worked with in the past, typically lasting only 3 months or less, have decided what I do "doesn't work", because they didn't get immediate results.

I don't want to work with that sort of, well, without wanting to sound harsh – stupidity. Do you think I got good at email marketing overnight? No way. I wrote daily emails for probably over a year or two, or even three before I'd say "I got good" at it.

So my point here is, I want to only work with the sort of person who's prepared to get involved, put some effort in, and work together so we'll generate spectacular results.

That drops you from the 1,000,000's to probably 100,000's.

So how do I identify the people I want to work with?

I spoke about this earlier, in defining your market. Specifically, you need to build an Avatar. I have two, I have the Avatar for the person I want to work with, and the Avatar for the person I don't want to work with.

It's not that I don't like, or respect those people - far from it. It's just that I have a specific type of person I *want* to work with. And that's OK (and also the whole point of this).

You don't *have* to work for everyone.

You don't *need* to work for everyone.

Build your avatar around the person who's the easiest to work with. The most profitable to work with. The most enjoyable to work with.

List demographics, be choosy. You could be as specific as this:

- Aged between 30-60 but probably on the older side
- Married, probably with kids
- Running business 5/10 years +
- Likes golf
- Enjoys reading
- Straight talking
- Enjoyable to share a drink with

And at the same time, you could then turn those attributes on their head to build the "Anti Avatar":

- Aged 18-30
- Probably single (although will explain more in a moment)
- New business, or struggling business
- Dislikes reading/learning new things
- Hides behind others, doesn't say what they really mean (so you don't know when stuff isn't really working)
- You try going for a drink but just end up sitting in silence......
or they can only talk about work.

Now it's important to say here, there's nothing wrong with these people, and everyone has to start a business somewhere and many people struggle (I know I have) BUT... that doesn't make them an ideal client *for me.*

Some of the traits annoy me, like hiding behind excuses or coming up with all sorts of reasons why they can't do something. When I say 'probably single', what I'm getting at here is I find it more important to target the married, family man – than I do anyone else. It's not that there's anything wrong with people who aren't married, far from it, but the point for me is, that I get on with 'married with kids' type folk, probably because that's what I am.

So let's recap. We've got to now identify four things:

1. What's your prospect's burning problem?

2. How/Why are you the solution?

3. What's your ideal avatar?

4. What's the opposite? Who do you NOT want to deal with?

So now, you should have a good idea of who you're targeting, what their pain points are, and how you can offer them a solution. Answer the four questions above, and you'll end up with something like this:

I am going to attract people to my business, by offering a solution to their burning problem [hint, when you write out yours, I mean to actually specify the solution/burning problem], and I'm going to do this in a number of ways. Either by being available in search results online, or by advertising in various places with headlines which attack their pain points and offer some sort of solution. That solution I'm advertising might be a guide, more information, or a consultation, but either way it'll be a tempting offer to the prospect because they really want their burning problem solved. Either way, paid advertising online and offline will bring people into my world, where I'll be able to then follow up with them, offering them the solution to their burning problem. I will also send offers to fix their burning problem via highly targeted direct mail. In summary, I am going to attract people to my business using a combination of media, by offering a solution to their burning problem.

Start Interrupting People

Part of your strategy, should not only include *how* to attract people into your world (although that's one of the *biggest* things you have to focus on) but you have to work out ways to interrupt them in their daily lives.

The reason for this in particular, is unlike 30 years ago (when I confess, I knew nothing of marketing other than Um Bongo adverts) we have so much information all the time, shoved in our faces these days, it's impossible to think without seeing an advert for "the new solution" or the "breakthrough we've been waiting for".

Classic example, of how much more advertising we're subjected to.

I'm going to a popular DIY store to get some bits for the garden... and Zach (my youngest, he's 6 at time of writing – that's important) came with me.

In the car, I was talking about how we're going to get some grass seed to make the garden look a bit healthier. "Oh! Daddy, if we're going to make the garden look better, we need <brand of weed killer>! Do you know why?"

Now for a minute, I was confused.

Why in the hell is my 6 year old telling me I need weed killer?

"Erm, no, why do we need <particular brand>?"

"Because it kills weeds DEAD!!! It gets RIGHT DOWN TO THEIR ROOTS!! Can you believe that? RIGHT DOWN TO THE ROOTS".

Now, I confess, I burst out laughing. Probably not the reaction he wanted, but basically, he'd seen an advert for this weed killer on his iPad so many times, it'd stuck in his head and he knew Garden = Weeds = this brand of weed killer.

Now you might be thinking "but Ben, this is just a classic case of advertising at work, albeit their demographic targeting was wrong" (or was it? I ended up buying it to stop him complaining we weren't buying it... huh....) but my point is, this is just one of a bazillion adverts they see every few minutes for the whole time they're playing the iPad (because they play a lot of 'free' games).

Now my kids don't get that much iPad time. They're limited, because <high horse> we're good parents </high horse> but our phones, tablets, laptops and computers are another medium where we've just accepted we're subjected to constant advertising. Facebook, every few posts is an advert, and often re-marketing (so advertising something you've seen online already) and there's a problem with this.

Here's the problem: We're used to seeing adverts so much more than we ever have been.

How often do you see an advert on Facebook? How often do you just scroll on by? How often do you suddenly stop in your tracks and go "Hey, this looks interesting...".

Not very often, I imagine. You're more interested in seeing cat or dog videos, right? (I know I am...). So we have to find better ways to interrupt our prospects. This means you have to either be extraordinarily creative with your Facebook/re-marketing, or come up with other ways to reach people.

Think: sending something out in the post.
Think: a phone call.
Think: an email.
Think: a message online (Facebook? LinkedIn? Depends what you like using).

As a rule, I don't like, or have, clients on my Facebook. Hell, I don't even want staff on my Facebook. There's a couple of exceptions, but I treat Facebook the very "old fashioned way", and I just have close friends/family on it.

It's just how I've run my Facebook forever, and I don't want to change it. I accept I'm very possibly missing out on some opportunities, but you know what? I don't really care. I don't care others do it, that's fine – it's just not for me.

But that doesn't mean I won't use it to advertise my business; I'll use it all day long to advertise. So here's the thing: You need a plan. A plan to interrupt.

What are you going to do to interrupt your prospects daily lives and get them thinking of you?

Facebook status? Image? Video? Facebook Live Video? LinkedIn Video? Email? Postcards? Letters? Text message?

Grab that notepad you used earlier, and jot down how you're going to go about interrupting your prospects. But here's a bigger problem. When you've decided how you're going to interrupt them, what are you going to say? There's only so many times you can say "my widget is cool, it does this and that and it costs £5".

You can come up with a fair few emails and messages over it, but ultimately… you just can't talk about the same ol' stuff day in day out. This is where you need to find new ways to reinforce your original message. Remember, your prospects have a burning problem, and your product/service is the solution to that. We've put ourselves in front of them when they were looking for a solution the first time, and we've got back in front of them again, and again, and again.

In comes the idea of 'story selling'. If you ever join my email list you'll experience this first hand, but just a few moments ago I was talking about Zach, and my trip to a DIY store. That exact story was used to sell tickets to my *Cork £100k Bootcamp* in 2018.

It's mixing a message about marketing, with a personal story that people will probably laugh at. But it doesn't matter how I deliver that message. I could stick it on Facebook, write it on a letter, hell I could tell the same thing over video (and you know what? I might do ALL of those things). The point is the message reinforces my point about marketing, and allows me at the end of it to offer a solution.

However you reinforce your message, make sure you inject your personality into it. The goal of what we're doing here, and the reason we're doing it, is to attract people who are like you and/or who like you. Think about your avatar. Those personality traits you've chosen are probably traits you yourself have, and subsequently you find it easier and more enjoyable to work with those people. So, make sure you attract the right person by putting your personality into your message.

Make The Offer Awesome

Part of any fundamental marketing strategy that's going to grow your business fast, is having a good offer. Now whilst your offer *should* be some sort of 'lead magnet' which *might* be an ebook, the way you offer that ebook is critical. For a start, everyone and their dog are now offering ebooks. You need your offer to be *special*. You need your offer to be *unique*.

But most importantly you need your offer to offer _value_.

Remember, just because it's free, doesn't mean you shouldn't sell it. You have to sell it like you were charging £1,000's for it. Because what you're asking for is valuable, it's their personal information and people are very protective of that (more so now than ever before).

So let's take a few minutes to think about your offer.

We bring people to you, and they're not ready to buy – but they're keen enough to give you some personal details in exchange for something.

What's it going to be?

I'll talk about Lead Magnets in depth later, and how to create them, but let's just say it's a Lead Magnet. It's a PDF, perhaps 10 pages, of information that your prospect is going to find valuable.

Let's assume for one minute, you're good at what you do, you must therefore have some good knowledge over your chosen subject. Whether that's IT problems, security, or how to rent a property… you have enough knowledge to put together a basic guide which is going to deliver some value to someone if they're interested in your topic. Right?

So let's just wave a magic wand and create this guide. There, it's done (honestly, I'll talk you through that later in the book).

Now what?

Well, let's go back to their burning problem.

You need to focus on their burning problem, and tempt them into downloading your guide because it contains information they need to know to fix it.

Something that you want to bear in mind is that people are lazy. They don't want to do it themselves half the time, or they already would have done. So they've got a problem they want fixed but they can't be bothered, so they're looking for a quick fix – hence your guide.

So you can give them the What, and the Why, and you can even give them the How. I remember years ago, I was told "Give them the What and the Why but charge for the How". I don't agree with that completely because, for the most part, people *can* do it themselves but they just don't *want* to.

So grab that notepad, and bring it all together. You should have your avatar, your prospect's burning problem, and your offer to solve that problem. In a nutshell, what you'll have there is your marketing strategy.

You'll have a document telling you everything you need to know. It'll tell you what their problem is, how to solve it, and specifically how *you* can help them solve it. All you need to do then, is translate that in to your website, and drive traffic to it.

That leads us very nicely into the next section of this book - your Website.

Writing Website Copy

So before I jump into how to write website copy (and in case you don't know what 'copy' means – it's just a term to refer to the sales text, i.e. in this case, the the text on the website) there's a very basic and fundamental set of rules that you need to follow.

Before I get to them let me ask you a question: How do you deal with an objection before it becomes an objection?

By objection, I mean quite simply someone objecting to part of your sales copy (which also might be verbal, if you're selling over the phone). The most typical objection is price because - well - that's normally the sticking point for a lot of people. And the objection of price is usually overcome by ensuring that you're not delivering price too soon, i.e. before you've defined enough value.

If someone is saying "that's too expensive" - then what they're really saying is "I can't see enough value or benefit".

And that is because you almost certainly haven't followed the copywriting rules, AIDA (Attention, Interest, Decision, Action). If you've read anything on writing sales copy in the past, you've probably heard of it, but this isn't a conversation - I can't just ask you and then move on assuming you know. You might have heard Desire (and hand on heart I don't know which is the 'true' meaning), instead of Decision, but really it's the same sort of effect. With enough desire, the decision is already made.

So let's talk about AIDA.

Pretty obvious, I guess, right? You've got to grab attention. This is almost always done with a strong compelling headline that attacks the problem at hand. A problem, essentially, equates to pain one way or another, and that's a good thing - because you can attack the pain/problem point in the headline, and thus capture their attention.

What you're doing is starting the slippery slope to the sale, because the whole purpose of any piece of sales copy is to get a sale, right?

And unless the whole piece of sales copy is read, it's unlikely to achieve that goal.

So you need to start by getting the headline read, and the sole purpose of that headline is to get the next line of copy read.

And the purpose of that line, is to get the next line of copy read.

And the purpose of that line … you get the idea, until before they know it, they're reading the call to action at the end, which basically is the answer to their problem. But let's not get carried away with ourselves.

My point here is, the headline grabs the attention, and the next lines grab their interest. As you progress through your sales copy, you need to keep their interest but you need to bring in the answer to their problem. You need to present a solution. That creates the desire.

And with a strong enough desire, as I said before, the decision is already made.

Ultimately everyone buys based on desire.

We all do it.

I do it.

I buy based on desire all too often. I want it, and I don't care what it takes for me to get it.

That's what your copy needs to achieve.

Each good piece of sales copy will have the structure of AIDA, but it will also have a compelling offer, with a reason to respond, but most importantly a reason to respond right now.

I'm pretty sure that for every piece of copy I've created, the ones that don't have the urgency behind responding (i.e. the reason to respond right now), have not performed anywhere near as well as those with a tight deadline or scarcity.

Scarcity works well but one thing I'd generally say with this is 'use it well'. For example, scarcity is saying there are only 10 spaces available, or 10 copies available, etc. You want to pick a figure that creates enough scarcity, but also doesn't sell yourself short.

In addition to that, you don't want to use false scarcity, people pretty much always see through it and it just ends up with you looking like an untrustworthy person.

I saw a campaign from a big Internet Marketer recently, who only had something like 200 spaces available. They claimed it was a fixed limit put in place by the venue and when spaces are gone, they're gone.

The deadline passed for early bookings, and a little while later they suddenly managed to "find" another 40 spaces.

It's so transparent it's pathetic.

Don't do it.

Writing website copy is not the easiest thing in the world. In fact most people underestimate it completely, and think that the essentials are to talk about yourself, what you do and how long you've been in business. I'll be honest, for years as a web designer I didn't realise quite how important it was either.

I would graphically design a website, make it look pretty, then ask them for content. This is actually a very stupid thing to do but it's what almost every single web designer will do today.

They'll assume the client has to provide the content, because, well, the client provides the content! That's just the way it is. I realised what a mistake this was a few years ago, and changed the rules. If I were to create you a website, I would write the copy for you.

It's almost unthinkable now that I would produce a website where I don't produce the copy. There's a small handful of exceptions, and those are where I've done websites for high end copywriters. I'm not a professional copywriter, although I am good.

What I mean by that is, I can write your website copy far better than you can.

I don't mean that in a condescending way, I simply mean that I've been writing so much copy, for so long, I understand what needs to be said and how it needs to be said in order to bring you the one thing you ultimately want: a return on investment.

But this isn't a sales pitch from me to you, this is a book enabling you to get the website you truly need. So what do I do? How do I write the copy? What are the main mistakes you need to avoid?

Many of these might sound obvious as you read them, but go to pretty much any standard small business website and I bet you you'll find the mistakes I'm talking about.

The Top Five Mistakes

Mistake One

The first, and possibly most common mistake I see in almost every single website, is that dreaded first line of text "Welcome to ...". Trust me, no-one wants to be "welcomed" to your website.

What they want, and more importantly need, is to know they're in the right place. This starts with a good, solid headline.

It should be a headline that focuses on the prospects pain or problem - as per our AIDA rules - and it should let them know immediately that they're in the right place because they're interested, and subsequently they will want to read on.

The 'takeaway' from this really is, that under no circumstance should you have a dominant headline on your website that is anything other than something that lets your reader know they're in the right place, and that you potentially have something to offer them that's going to help them 'fix' their problem.

Mistake Two

This mistake is probably just as common, if not more common, than mistake one. It's a close run between this and mistake number one...

And I say it's just as common because actually, even if you've triggered that you shouldn't welcome people to your website, writing against this style I'm about to talk about is very difficult.

I know that, personally, It has taken me years to change my style.

It's not something you can instantly 'switch' and I've often spent hours at a keyboard trying to think of ways to word something differently, so that I'm not doing it.

The mistake?

It's 'weeing all over your website'. We do this, we do that, etc. But it's more complex than that, because sometimes, even if you're trying to convey the benefits of what you do, conveying those without writing 'we' is really difficult.

It's one of the prime reasons that I insist on writing the copy for the websites we produce (aside from me trying to make the client's life easier).

For example "We write all your copy for you". Kind of sounds OK right? I mean, strictly speaking I'm conveying a benefit. I'm telling the prospect that they won't have to write any content, and subsequently they have more free time and less hassle.

So why not write that in the first place?

Firstly, it's not instinctive.

Secondly, you look at every other website and every other website says "we do this" etc. So you're almost trained to write in a certain way because of the websites you've been looking at for years.

So it's counter-intuitive to write "Don't worry about a thing, all the copy is written for you and you can just put your feet up and relax".

Same meaning, but different message, right?

Mistake Three

The third mistake I often see is to put that all-important copy into a carousel. You know what I mean, right? The sliding images or similar across the screen. If you have your copy built into something like that, what you're doing is irritating your readers/prospects.

I know this from past irritations myself, where I've been quite interested in something but then the picture changes and so does the text.

It's seriously annoying but, more importantly, it's going to cause confusion unless the copy is unrelated to the rest of the website. And if it's unrelated to the rest of the website, what good is it actually doing?

Is it contributing to your AIDA?

It won't be, if it's unrelated.

The copy on your website should not be focused on you, it should be focused on your reader. It should be focusing on the benefits of what you provide, and giving them a reason to get in touch (refer back to the AIDA rules if you need to).

Mistake Four

A big mistake I see far, far too often is, that the copy is actually OK, but there's something crucial missing from it.

I don't know why web designers think it's acceptable - even from an uneducated age I believed there always had to be a call to action.

But I see it time and again and it drives me up the wall, especially when it's actually something I want. I can't find the way to take the 'next step' - whether that's enquiring/signing up or whatever.

Sometimes, depending on how badly I want the product (which I guess would mean their copy structure is good) I will hunt for as long as it takes … but most of the time?

I guess you know what I'd do, you'd probably do the same.

You click back, and find someone else.

Mistake Five

The fifth mistake (and it's by no means the last, but perhaps the final of what are the 'bigger' mistakes) is inconsistent flow.

By that I mean, perhaps you'll read the headline, but because the copy doesn't flow well or it's not laid out right, the 'story' doesn't make sense.

I've both done this myself and seen it a million and one times on websites. I remember a critique I had done around four years ago, which pointed out that my headline, and what was the next line of readable copy, were completely inconsistent.

At the time I almost felt like disputing it but once I really sat down and looked, I realised it was really stupid of me.

The thing is, with poor layout, even if you've got things written in an ordered way, they can read out of order, or not make sense.

It's one of the reasons that most websites I produce now are single column, and the text flows down in a solid line with headlines and paragraphs of text matched together. And I think that that is the reason our websites perform for our clients better than ever.

A Bigger Problem...

Getting your website sales copy right is important, and how it's structured is really important to the success of any marketing campaign you'll run to it.

Beyond the "welcome to my website" type mistakes though, another big mistake people tend to make is, that they completely and utterly ignore Attention and Interest and move straight on to either Decision or Action.

Obviously, they're not doing this consciously. I'd suggest that only a relatively small number of business owners are even *aware* of AIDA in the first place.

The point is, most people who arrive at your 'point of sale' are not in the position to buy and are in fact, ready to run the opposite way when you ask for their credit card details.

They're completely unconvinced by your product, or they think it's too expensive because they haven't been convinced of the benefit. This is why most sales pages convert at less than 1%, meaning 99 out of every 100 people that come to your sales page leave without buying.

So how do you capture more people, and how do you get a better rate of sales? Well, as I'm sure you've worked out by now - you need to capture their attention first.

You start off with a headline that significantly talks to your reader. It should attack a problem or pain they're experiencing. You don't want to be focusing on yourself, which is the mistake almost all business owners make when building a website.

I mentioned in the five things to avoid, that the most common mistake I see time and again is "Welcome to…". To be blunt, who really wants to be welcomed to a website? Do *you*? Really? Honestly? Do you ever really think "Wow, they welcomed me, I feel special". No! Quite simply it's just the easy way to start writing something, because it's what everyone else does, so it feels right. But just because everyone else does it, doesn't mean it's right.

So you're writing a headline that captures their attention because it's focusing on a problem or pain.

"But I sell X, how the hell can I find a pain from that?"

Take a company like Apple, and let's look at the iPhone. The iPhone is a luxury item, and at no point has anyone 'needed' an iPhone to continue functioning as a human being.

But it's easy to see how Apple create a pain point.

They have defined themselves as a high end luxury goods company, and created an ethos whereby if you don't own the latest Apple device you're somehow cheap or inferior.

The pain point for your widget, as it could be with Apple, is as simple as defining how much more awesome your life would be with the widget, and thus, by not owning it, your life would suck.

If you're serving business to business, stop focusing on what you're selling and think about it this way - what if you were to focus on the *end benefit* of your service? Perhaps what you do frees up enough time to ensure that the prospective customer has more time and money in their business?

You're not selling a service, you're selling an increase of productivity for their business. You're not selling a widget, you're selling a better, more enjoyable life.

You're selling the benefit. Remember those words?

"What's In It For Me"

Now, I'm sure you're getting the message by now that 'sell by the benefit' is the sure-fire way to grow your sales fast, because as you now know 'nobody cares about you'.

It's one of those moments of realisation, I think, that transforms your marketing speak forever. I know it took me quite some time to 'get it', even after listening to that seminar over a decade ago.

And as I hammer it home, time and time again, I know that eventually you'll 'get it' too. And suddenly you'll look at 'about us' pages and roll your eyes.

I remember the first time I heard the term, one of my clients simply referred to it as "someone has wee'd all over your website".

"We do this ...", "we do that ..." etc.

So, I hear you ask, how do you write sales copy that really wins? Is it just about the benefit? Well, kind of...

So back to AIDA - the 'copywriting formula'. Fundamentally, this is what it all comes down to.

I guess you could say 'bringing it all together' is the key. You have to really focus in hard on each element of AIDA and make sure your copy punches each one of those criteria.

Let's start at the beginning and look at Attention again... We're all familiar with clickbait headlines, right? Those stupid, no, ridiculous headlines that just create an instant desire to click. It's irresistible. The trouble is, they have 'limited lifespan', because the people that see it and click on it, are often left disappointed.

You know it's going to be something that is nowhere near as interesting as the headline describes, so you don't end up clicking.

Effectively, you've lost the trust of your reader. And that is game over.

So I don't want you to make crazy promises you can't keep, when it comes to the headline and the rest of the copy.

You want it to be a pretty eye grabbing headline, obviously, but don't deceive the reader. If we then take our attention over to Interest, this is actually (ha) quite interesting.

You see, it's more than just writing interesting content. I've seen really interesting topics butchered by depressingly boring copy.

So the key is, to write in a way so that the reader doesn't realise they've read half the article. Or the entire article. The goal is to make use of the 'slippery slope' strategy ... that is to say, the purpose of the headline is to get them to read the first line of the content.

The purpose of the first line of content is to get them to read the second line of content. The purpose of the second line ... you get the idea. It's referred to as the slippery slope to the sale, because suddenly your reader is reading your sales material rather than your interesting story or similar. One of the keys to writing good copy, which I think most people overlook, is the actual 'style' of writing.

You should write like you speak when you write your emails in your email marketing, and in fact the same goes for when you're writing a sales letter or any piece of marketing material.

The most successful sales letters I write, are written like I am writing to a friend. Well, they're conversational at least (written in the same format as this book, for example).

But it's obvious why they're successful, because people don't want a 'sales letter', but they do like a letter that's written to them personally.

And the thing is, that can still be a great sales letter even though it doesn't appear to be. So we know we want to write to them 'personally', and we want to grab their attention with a good headline, and then we want to write in an informal, conversational style. It's worth saying here, because I know this has come up from time to time, by conversational I don't mean that you have to write about your personal life.

You simply have to keep the letter written as if you were speaking to that person ... because, well, you are speaking to that person.

The medium might be paper, instead of voice, but you're still going to need to say the same things, and if you sat and had a conversation with a prospective client and spoke like a traditional sales letter - you wouldn't get very far, would you?

The client would get bored pretty quick, and most likely confused too.

You've got to remember, whilst everything you do is so mundane and every-day to you, to your prospective customer it's quite possibly extraordinarily complicated and/or scary.

I don't mean talk to them like they're idiots, obviously, but to a large extent you've got to talk to them like they have no idea what you're on about.

Address their pain, face on, and start to provide answers and solutions.

Sales copy comes down to this: people want more money and more free time. Whilst that might sound a little basic, that's as simple as it gets.

So if your product gives them something they want, that makes their life easier and brings them closer to one of those things, then you're on to a winner.

Pain is the focus point here. Most business owners invest £1000's upon £1000's on their online marketing. That might just be a website, it might be a Google campaign, it might be Facebook, whatever.

For many business owners, online marketing just isn't successful, because they're doing it in a misinformed way and, frankly the vast majority of Web Designers out there have no clue when it comes to direct response marketing. This isn't a sales pitch for me, by the way, I'm just saying that I can identify that point very easily.

Just the other day I was talking to a new client and he was telling me how he'd been through revision after revision of his website, but realised his web designer had no comprehension of direct response marketing. And in fact, when he challenged him on that, the web designer said "you're the only one that asks me to do things this way".

Wow, I mean, just focus on that for a minute, right?

Because that's not uncommon.

If you start doing your marketing in a direct response orientated way and focus on pain/how you can fix that pain, and write everything with AIDA in mind... Well, your competition will wonder WTF you're doing and why the hell you're so busy.

To summarise, when you're writing your copy, focus on their pain and describe the benefit of what you're doing.

To spell it out for you, from a web design perspective, you could say something along these lines:

Finally, you can get a lead generating website that looks great, automates your sales process and delivers you sales, giving you more time to spend at home with the family.

Now I've not put a great deal of thought into that, but that still sounds a load better than the typical:

We'll develop you a beautiful bespoke design website that looks great and reflects how professional you really are.

The latter doesn't really convey any real *benefit* other than you might end up with a pretty looking website, compared to one that's actually going to make you money.

I've seen copy like that all too often, and truth be told, I used to write copy like that! As I've said a few times, I'm not professing to have always been amazing at what I do, because it takes experience and practice to get good at things, and I've been gaining experience and practicing for many years now.

It's frustrating, when you write a huge sales letter, or huge sales email, or advert, or landing page (or, well, anything) and then you get it critiqued and you're told "it's all wrong".

The temptation is to run it anyway, which I've done ... and I've paid the price (literally) for it.

So believe me when I say, when you're writing your sales copy, make sure you focus on the benefit, attack their pain, offer the solution (which creates the desire) and always, always, always,

always, have a strong call to action.

Social Proof

This section is really hugely important for the success of your online campaign. "Social proof" that your product works, reassures people. The trouble is – it's become so common place to have testimonials on your site now, that it becomes questionable as to whether they're trustworthy or not.

If you're Business To Business – then this becomes a slightly easier problem to solve. You can, (usually with the customer's permission!), leave the customer's name and company name alongside the testimonial, making it feel more authentic and also – should the potential customer wish – verifiable.

If you're Business To Consumer – then the only way to truly get around this (and this is great for B2B as well) is to use video testimonials. This is significantly harder to get done – but is less frequently implemented by your competitors – so the more you can source and put on your website the better. Really simple, face to camera style "I bought X and it totally solved my problem Y, and the person Z from the company was brilliant". Five or six of those on your website and your conversions will dramatically increase.

The advantage of having video testimonials is that, as well as embedding them on to your website, you can host them on YouTube, which is of course the world's second biggest search engine.

The benefit of this is that you can include keywords around the problem your product solves, and people can get a first-hand recommendation before they even visit your website.

How many testimonials should you have? Well, as many as possible but how you structure that is important. You don't want people scrolling through pages and pages of recommendations otherwise the call to action loses focus. It's best, if you can, if you can slide through a few different testimonials, but if you've got video then you could group some in between some sales/promotional material (i.e. you could develop a video which talks about your product, combines some animation, and also some customer testimonials).

Just to mention as well, sometimes the word "testimonials" doesn't quite fit with the image you want on your website, which is fine. You can go with Customer Comments, Feedback or even Case Studies.

A strong case study with a customer comment can work wonders for conversion ratios, as people are able to see a full in depth analysis of what you've done, and the fact that the customer is happy.

Chapter Three:
Your Website

Who would have thought, sixty years ago we'd have all been completely dependent on computers. Or even thirty years ago, that our lives would be entirely orientated around the Internet as we know it today? And who would have thought that twenty years ago, just as mobiles were really becoming fiercely popular, that these handheld devices would one day be used for the Internet *more* than a desktop PC?

Now, I consider myself lucky.

We've all heard of Generation X, and Millennials, but there's an in-between. So called Xennials. I do find the whole thing a bit ridiculous *but* it actually serves a purpose. Let's say you're born in 1975. Technically you're "labelled" as Generation X.

Now consider you're born in 1985, you're considered a Millennial. That is, by the time you'll be reaching adulthood it will be around the year 2000.

But because of the rapid technology growth we saw in the late 90s and early 2000's, a divide within that group has appeared.

That's because those that were born say, from 1985, had vastly superior technology available (because of its exponential growth) than those born in say, 1980.

So a new group was defined. The Xennial. This definition was almost *required* if you consider what people deem by the labels "Generation X" and "Millennial". Generation X grew up without technology, and Millennials with.

I'll come back to this in a second, but the thing is, Millennials get a bad rap because people consider them to be lazy and entitled. But *every* generation has lazy buggers who want to do nothing but complain and live off the state. It's nothing new. It's just, there's *more* of them now than ever before.

Go find a population growth over time graph. Look at it over 2,000 years. It's scary.

Let's just look at the last couple of hundred years though. Let me quote some figures: In 1804, the global population was estimated to be around 1 billion people. Around 150 years later, in 1951, global population figures sat at 2.5 billion people.

That doesn't sound too bad, does it? Over 150 years to 2.5x the population. Think of advances in science, medicine, etc, and it's no real surprise.

But by 1971, it had already grown to 3.7 billion people. That's an extra 2.2bn people in just 20 years. Eek. By 1991, we were up another 1.7 billion people and the global population stood at 5.4 billion. Let's scoot forward to today, and at the start of 2019 the global population stood at an estimated 7.7bn.

So it took 150 years to multiply the population by 2.5, but in only 68 years, the World's population had basically tripled.

(I am going somewhere with this so stay with me…)

That's a lot more lazy buggers. But it's also a lot more honest, hard working, business owners all trying to make it in the World and to take control of their own future. I'm not going to argue that environmental changes over the last 30 years hasn't made an impact on people's behaviours and attitudes because clearly it has. But the sheer increase in people itself, has an impact on how people go about living their lives.

Think about the logistics of it, health care systems, policing, education. It's all vastly more complex now than it was 68 years ago. Not just because of technological advances but because of the volume of people.

Scaling up is always hard.

Now I'm sure I could go off on a tangent here, and start discussing about how we're going to have to colonise planets like Mars to sustain our growth…. But I'll sidestep that and return to my original point.

Run a business in 1951? You would have had a lot less competition than today. Because not only were businesses largely constrained to their local areas (with the exception of national press, and television/radio, which were prohibitively expensive for most businesses) in some ways, it was probably pretty easy. Assuming you had a good product to sell.

But we're not in 1951, and the Internet has revolutionised how we both shop for products, and research for services. Let's return to my original point, I feel I'm quite lucky.

I grew up in the 80's and 90's, but was born *just* early enough to remember life as a child completely free from technology (as we know it today). But I was old enough to witness the growth first hand. To see the rise of the Internet, to see the Dotcom bubble, to experience the revolution of mobile technology first hand.

All whilst having the opportunity of growing up outside, entertaining ourselves with decks of cards because there was literally *nothing else*. Having phone conversations with friends, over the one fixed phone in the house because *it was the only way*.

You might be asking yourself why this is relevant at all to Internet marketing, and more specifically - your website, and here's the most important point: people of my generation and older, have been slow to adopt mobile technology, but more and more *are*.

People of my generation and younger, have known nothing *but* technology, and more specifically mobile technology. An 18 year old today (as I write this, 2019), would have been 11 in 2012, and in 2012 the iPhone had been out for 5 years.

To put it in real terms, as a parent you're concerned for your child's safety, so when they first start going to senior school and more specifically, going out 'on their own' - well, you'll want to give them a phone, won't you? You need to be able to contact them and make sure they're safe.

And so to the crux of the matter.

Your website, and online marketing, absolutely <u>must</u> be mobile orientated. Not just to please the young 'uns, far from it, in fact.

Let me make the point again.

People who were born in the mid 80's and beyond have known nothing but technology, and being that they have known nothing but technology, are very good at using it.

People who were born before the late 70's have, as adults, seen technology grow. But because they haven't grown up with it, it's not <u>natural</u> to them. It's why it's almost a cliche nowadays, "I just have to fix my mum's computer".

It's difficult to consider an analogy that would be the inverse, but the one thing I *will* say about millennials is, they don't know how lucky they are. As someone who was born in between the eras, I have the benefit of seeing both ends of the stick.

All this means, mobile traffic now far exceeds that of desktop.

That means if your website isn't mobile optimised, and I mean that in a way that means more than just 'responsive' – then you're going to be frustrating and losing visitors.

So let's cover what 'responsive' means first. Responsive simply means that the website 'responds' to the size of the browser, it essentially shrinks down to the size of the screen but keeps things like the text size the same, so that it's readable and easy to navigate.

But that's just the technical side of it.

Being mobile friendly is so, so much more than that. I've seen mobile sites which leave the logo at full size (or at least 100% width) and it ends up taking up half the mobile screen.

Stupid, right?

Opt-In Marketing

The question is, with your website and your marketing, "How

soon should you *sell* to someone?" And the answer? Well, that depends. If someone has typed in to Google "buy gadget model ABCZ1" then take them to a page to sell them that gadget. But that's one of the few times I'd take someone to a direct sales page.

In almost every other scenario, you want to look at starting a relationship with your prospective customer, not trying to get a sale.

But the vast, *vast* majority of websites have the same old call to action. "Get a call back", or "Get a free quote", or "Get a free consultation". Don't misunderstand me, you absolutely *should* make it possible for someone to get in touch, or get a quote - but probably 99% of your website visitors won't be in the position to buy.

They're just researching, investigating, looking up suppliers or ideas. The point is, the majority of people you'll have visit your website will leave, and never come back.

Why?

Because the only thing you had to offer them was a free quote. And that's boring. You need to focus on building a relationship.

You might think, "I only sell sellotape, how can I build a relationship?"

It doesn't matter what your industry is, what you provide or how you provide it. You can always offer advice to people around what you sell, or around the problem that what you sell solves.

Think about a guide "The 10 types of sellotape you didn't know existed for all kinds of tasks". OK I might be pushing my luck there, but I'm sure you can see my point. What I'm really trying to stress here is that, pretty much the biggest myth flying around, and the one that retailers fall for all the time, is people use the Internet to buy.

Yes – people *do* buy on the Internet, but that's not what they *primarily* use it for. You might be thinking "Don't be crazy, I buy online all the time!" – but think very carefully about your day, from morning to evening.

How much time do you spend reading the news? On Facebook? On a forum or maybe a hobby related website? How often do you think "I think I'll buy one of those" – then Google it to find out more information. I hate to admit it, but I spend probably at least 12 hours a day 'online'. Much less at the weekend for sure, but even so the figures are probably still quite high.

My point is that conversion rates wouldn't be so low on an industry average if more people solely used the Internet to buy, but the fact is, people want more information on something they are often just *considering* purchasing.

You might be searching around online to compare prices for something you're about to buy in the high street, or be searching around online for the best deal. This can tie in with 'bundling' other products with the main product to make the initial product look like it has a better offer.

Think about double glazing, or a new car. People will spend a significant amount of time researching online, before finally making a decision and buying.

So, how do we make use of this traffic?

What's the point?

If they're coming to your site to find out a bit of information what can we do? How can we take a conversion rate from 2% up to 20%? If you'll remember, the conversion rate is simply the number of people in 100 that 'convert' from a visitor to a lead, or a sale (if you're e-commerce).

The best way to increase your conversion rate, is to focus on building a relationship instead of a sale. And one of the best ways to start a relationship online is to give something away. After all, if people are looking for information, why not give it to them?

I don't mean giving part of your service or product away like a free trial, as that can devalue your product/service. But giving a free report or guide is a great way to start a relationship, and far more effective than the typical common tactic to try and extract personal details in the form of "join our newsletter".

Think of the number of sites you see which have "Join our newsletter for updates".

Who cares?

Really?

If you're constantly expanding your products and services then you could look at offering an update on "upcoming new products which will solve your problem of X by doing Y" – but this still isn't enough generally to convince (enough) people to give you their personal details.

And by that I mean to make the Pay Per Click cost effective.

Because we're doing this, through Pay Per Click, right? Right.

People hate junk email / spam, and hate being harassed.

Quite often, if they will fill out a form online, that's exactly what they expect will happen – they will be harassed. So how do we handle this?

This will, of course, vary completely depending on what you do, but take a few examples:

Travel Agent: Download our free guide on 'How to get the most out of Orlando'

Estate Agent: Download our free guide on 'How to get the maximum price for your property'

E-commerce: Download our guide on 'How to make the right Rug choice for your room'

There are hundreds of different opportunities no matter what your market and no matter what you're selling. A free information guide is great, and if you can, look at getting some printed.

It only needs to be a few pages, and these can be produced at really low cost. You could produce them in-house to trial it initially, but I'd recommend getting them done professionally – this will be the first thing your potential customer gets from you, so you want to make sure it's the right quality.

Also, if you send it out in the post, rather than as a downloadable PDF – you're increasing the likelihood it will actually be read. You'll decrease your initial conversion rate, because people will have to give you their address, but in the long run, the physical address is far more valuable. You then have their address - so you're able to co-ordinate your online marketing with some direct mail.

The thing is because so many people offer downloads here and there, your download will be lost within their 'downloads folder' or desktop. If you have a booklet on their desk, or at home, it sits much more in their focus.

Don't just be sending sales letters or trying to sell through the post. The aim of this process is to build a long term relationship where the potential customer sees you as a source of information – an authority on your subject.

Going back to the 'Newsletter' idea, this is rubbish for Email but works quite well for Direct Mail. You can incorporate special offers, but also bring a complete personal touch.

How many of your competitors would send 2-3 pages of written content along with just one special offer for a product?

It used to be that years ago, you would look at 7 points of contact to a sale. You would write a letter, make a telephone call, write a letter, make a telephone call, etc. This process could also take much longer.

As I was saying earlier on, over the last 10-20 years, our lives have changed so much with the introduction of the Internet in our daily lives, and with the constant flow of sales messages hitting our inboxes all day – this process has grown significantly. You're now looking at up to 28 points of contact or more for a sale. This might seem like an absolutely impossible task, but this will lead really nicely into our next section – Email marketing.

It doesn't matter if you've got this lovely new website (or maybe you've got a rubbish website, hey I'm not one to judge) if no matter how much you advertise it you just don't get the leads or sales.

Now again I'm playing blind here, maybe you've thrown a few hundred at it, or maybe thousands … but if I know one thing, and I know it well – it's that most business owners have their website set up all wrong, and don't get the return on investment they want, and in many cases, so desperately need.

It's been the destruction of business after business, which is another topic in itself (why not to rely on online only) but even if you're generating leads offline, you still need a good website – it's a great facilitator of form filling and the like (essentially – 'lead capture').

Now, I don't want to make this all about me, but you need some background. I've been helping people with their websites for over a decade now and things have changed a lot over the last ten years. But I can tell you this too – I've learnt a lot along the way. The sort of website I produced ten years ago looks very different to the websites I produce today – but probably not for the reasons you're thinking.

Sure, twenty years ago websites were all horrible.

They were ugly by today's standards, they were often lacking in any kind of remotely useful functionality, and even the good ones were still pretty poor. Actually, I say 'ugly' but around twenty years ago (in the early 2000's) there was like a mini-revolution in web design, and they started to look pretty cool. Companies with a lot of dosh to splash around had some pretty snazzy designs and I'm pleased to say the designs I put out back then were still pretty good by today's standards.

But the majority of small business owners websites were terrible. I know this because it was my business model back then to find companies with terrible websites and offer them a better one (something I sort of do now, to be fair).

But some of the businesses had realised how important online would be (especially after the 'dot com' boom and even after the bust), and had put a lot of effort into designing fancy looking websites and/or adding in a ton of functionality. Two years prior to starting my business I was a full time web developer working full time on a single website.

So I knew that websites could contain a bucket load of useful information, and could be places of e-commerce, but what I didn't really twig at the time was, that they could really be used as sources of leads - at least not in the sense that I'm going to talk to you about.

A lead, as I considered it, was someone who enquired specifically about the product/service on offer. They were ready to buy, and if they didn't buy, you didn't speak to them again. That's the mistake that a lot of business owners still make now. Despite vast quantities of information around the Internet and more than ever before about Direct Response marketing and automated follow up - most business owners I come into contact with haven't got any sort of continuous follow up system in place.

So if the way a website is structured (but most importantly what's on offer) is so fundamentally crucial to the success of a website, it's no wonder that almost all small business websites fail completely if they have the wrong offer.

So what should be offered?

How should it be structured?

Let's dig into that in more detail, but just before I do, remember: Your website should be focused on the prospective client, not you and not your business (you know, focusing on the problem of the reader, rather than "we've been in business 25 years"). But most important of all, it should offer something of value to the prospective customer/client, in return for something of value too, perhaps their contact details or similar.

Above The Fold

I have talked about how essentially brand itself is less relevant. I don't want to insinuate that branding isn't relevant because it is. There's a fine line to draw between making sure your website and marketing has a consistent brand message, and how important your logo is.

You see big brands changing their logos all the time, don't you? Sometimes it's a big change, sometimes it's a small change, or sometimes it's a huge change, where they change the name completely, as well as their logo/imagery.

But very quickly, you'll see that *everything* changes. Their branding throughout all their marketing changes to align itself to their new logo.

My point is, your logo itself, doesn't matter. Stop worrying about it. Stop fussing over green or blue, yellow or green, although, do avoid red. Perhaps more importantly, stop fussing over whether the line should be just to the left, or just to the right, or underneath.

It. Doesn't. Matter.

Not to your average Joe, reading your landing page, finding out more information on whatever it is they're looking for. What they want, is a simple, straight forward and easy to understand web page that gives them all the content they want.

Sure, they want it to look nice.

And sure, they want the branding to look lovely.

But those last two points are far, far less important than the first

- that you deliver content.

So if we talk about how your website itself should look, if we talk about your overall design for your homepage, for example, what do we consider to be the most important points?

I always look at this from the top down. I don't remember where I heard it first, but the phrase 'above the fold' is important. It refers to broadsheet newspapers, which should be quite tall in length and folded half way. They're stacked so you can only see the top half. Therefore, the top half must be damn compelling to you - otherwise they won't sell many.

So let's look at the 'above the fold', and consider the main factors. First, you should now know that your logo size needs to be a fraction of what it probably is, because no-one cares about your logo. It's always important to have a phone number at the top, and this is especially true with mobile, so aligned to the right of the logo you should have either a call back button or phone number, depending on whether or not you actually want your phone number publicly displayed.

Then, pretty much directly under that you want ... you guessed it – the headline. This should take up no more than a quarter of the screen, with your first couple of lines of copy directly under that. If you can, have a call to action visible too. You want to ensure that this looks good on both the larger more 'premium' phones and the mid-range phones.

Ultimately phones are all relatively similar when it comes to screen size and browsers, and you want to make sure it looks OK on a smaller screen too, but if you're targeting the "upper end" of the market (which you should be) then you can guess they're probably going to have a larger screen.

Other mobile considerations are things like contact forms. You've got to make it easy. Make use of mobile-specific fields, i.e. you can code it so that when you press into the field, if it's a number, you get a proper number keypad.

It's all about making it easy.

Don't you hate it, when you're doing your level best to give someone your details, because you *want* the call back, but the website's just not working right? I don't know how many times I've been in that situation but it's a lot.

So when it comes to your contact forms, I'd suggest that you make sure that when you're having a call to action (such as 'click here' to get a call back) then you take them to a separate page, not a 'popover' form. If you don't know what I mean by popover form, it's simply where the main screen sort of blacks out, then you have the form pop up in the middle.

These are fine and dandy on a desktop, and they're OK on a mobile if you're only asking for a couple of fields and there's not too much else on there, but if it involves scrolling it can be really buggy and VERY frustrating on a mobile.

I've given up many a time trying to fill in forms like that, and on some where I've been determined, it's only because I've played around for a while that I've managed to actually get it so that I could hit the submit button.

But the thing is, people are fickle. People are insanely fickle…. And if you cause ANY reason for people to get frustrated, you'll be losing enquiries, and that's an absolute guarantee. I stopped using pop over forms on our landing pages years ago now, and it was a simple decision to make.

It was obvious, on one of our key clients, we removed the pop over and enquiries were up by a significant margin (at least 20-30% in the first few months, and continued to rise). But I must stress, keep the forms easy to fill out. Resist the need to make it look fancy, when simple will do.

Focus on your offer, and make it obvious what you want people to do. Remember, they might have to scroll on a phone, and it might not be obvious they have to scroll. Imagine your user has just fallen out of the sky and has no idea how to use a phone... Design your form around that, and you'll do well.

Before we move on to a very crucial topic we should consider one last thing. This is a question I want you to ask yourself, not because the answer is so stupidly obvious, but because we often forget the answer:

Do people behave the same on a mobile as they do on a desktop, and does that impact the offers that we make?

Well, let me answer the question of 'do people behave the same' by throwing that out to you. Do *you* behave the same on your mobile as you do on your desktop? Of course you don't. It's almost so obvious that it doesn't need stating, but I'm going to state it because people seem to be completely oblivious.

If you're on a desktop, and you're applying for, or purchasing something that requires a fair few details - you're going to be relatively receptive to a large form with lots of fields.

It's probably a bit of a turn off, and it might be a bit overwhelming, but it's nothing when compared to presenting the same form on a mobile. It'll cost you a few enquiries, if you have a really convoluted form on desktop - but it'll cost you hundreds if you're on a mobile.

People want it to be *easy*.

So let's take the worst case scenario, and just say you need in the region of 30 or 40 fields as part of your process. Put all that on one page on a PC, and you might get people filling it out (you really should break it up in to stages though).

Put it on a mobile and people will run for the hills.

The answer? Make it mobile friendly, of course. That starts with an adjustment that'll help you with desktop conversions too -

breaking it up into steps. There's a few times where I've had reason to request upwards of 30-40 fields of information for an enquiry (for a client) and this means the whole process has to be super smooth.

But the first step out of all of this is just to take 5/10 pieces of information at a time, before going to the next stage. This works the same on e-commerce - with a client recently we simply sat down and made a note of all the relevant fields required for an order. Then - rather than going with what the e-commerce platform wanted us to do, we re-structured the whole thing so it asked for the information in a logical and sensible order - but broken up over four different steps.

Second, make the input fields give the right 'keyboard' for the job. If you're asking for a number, make sure a number pad pops up. If you're asking for an email, make sure the input field is a type of 'email' so that the @ sign is present on the screen.

You're quite probably thinking "I have NO IDEA how to do that, you're talking gibberish you fool". Yes, I accept these are technical details but they're crucial if you want a form to be filled in on your website.

So you need do nothing more than throw this book at your web designer and/or relay those instructions above.

But more importantly, you need to fill out the form yourself and not rest until it's the easiest form to fill out in the world.

Whatever call to action you're asking people to make, if you're asking them to do it on a mobile, keep it as simple and easy as you possibly can.

What should your website do?

So it's all easy to get carried away with talking about what a website shouldn't do, and talk about all the wrong ways to do things… but that's like watching one of those reality TV shows isn't it? Like the one where they take on an apprentice… can't quite think what it's called… but seriously, in those shows there's always a bunch of people who can find the reasons you *shouldn't* do something or shouldn't have done something, but they're the last to suggest what you actually *should* do.

So what exactly should a website do? Good question, I'm glad you asked.

The ultimate aim of your website should be one thing and one thing only: to make you more money.

A website that simply 'looks good', or is there for a point of information, is pointless. I know countless companies I've come into contact with over the years, that don't want their website to operate as a lead source because they weren't happy with the type of leads they got from their website.

Someone I knew from a networking group, who ran a financial advice firm, specifically said to me: "I don't want Internet leads because they're just scammers, or it's just rubbish". Now I wanted to help him out, but the thing is, when you have a web designer telling you that you just need a better website to get better quality leads (which is what I was saying), you simply think they're trying to sell to you for their own benefit (I wasn't).

If I'd written a book on the subject at the time, I'd have handed him a copy, but this was well before my first book.

All it really meant of course, was that they hadn't qualified their leads properly. Or more likely, their targeting was simply way off - in the sense that it was non-existent. They had probably, at best, only ever had 'organic' enquiries. That is to say, they hadn't tried any pay per click.

If you're running pay per click, but you're still getting too many 'crappy' leads - then *that's* where you ramp up the qualification process, or tighten your targeting. If you have a proper questionnaire/application form or similar you'll find the leads you get are actually significantly better. It makes sense, however, that the more information you ask for, the fewer enquiries you get. So it's a balance.

Now I know I said that your website should do just one thing – make you more money... But it can and should do more than that, it should help build your authority and positioning. These are two things I'll cover separately.

So first of all is authenticity; I see website after website that just looks shoddy. It looks amateurish at best, and you're left wondering if the company is even in business still. Quite often they are, and have no idea just how bad their website is making them look.

Let me be clear, I'm not saying you should go out and spend £10,000's on a luxury looking website with fancy images all over, just to get 'authenticity' – but I am saying that you should at least treat your website in the same light as any other piece of marketing you would want to put out. It should be high quality and it should reflect the level of professionalism you / your company offer.

Whilst I can understand the temptation to use the DIY website companies, I would strongly recommend against doing so. There's a few reasons for me saying this, and it's not to fuel the industry of web designers. Honestly, most web designers don't have a clue about marketing and have no real understanding of Return On Investment either. They'll just stare at you like a deer in the headlights whilst they try and come up with some jargon to distract you.

So you need to find a good balance; you want a website that looks professional, but you don't want it all to be about pretty pictures and just looking fancy. It should focus on the reader, not you. Remember, I've talked about before, that if you even contemplate writing "Welcome to my website" you need a slap on the wrists. If that's on your website right now - don't worry. I know it's not your fault, you're probably just copying the competition *or* you've let your web designer write the content, but believe me, the competition and/or web designer is WRONG.

I've already talked about how you have literally just seconds before people make a subconscious decision as to whether they're in the right place or not, and welcoming people and talking about how many years you've been in business is the fastest way to lose visitors.

Instead, focus on having a headline that really talks to your potential clients, draws some interest and compels them to read further. How do you do this? Not with a logo, I can tell you that much. Every time I hire a new designer, I get the same objections in their training period.

"But the logo can't be that small!" – Oh yes… it *can*.

Ultimately you want to minimise distractions and draw in the reader's focus to your strongest possible piece of material – your headline.

When I first really got to grips with this, I have to admit, the websites I produced did look pretty crap. They were bland, and often lacked the authenticity I'm talking about here (but that being said, still generated good quality leads because they were focused on the right things). Over the years I've come to realise that yes, a page that looks entirely bland can and does work, but not as a homepage for your website.

There are ways, which we'll explore further in this guide, that mean you really can get the best of both worlds. An attractive and professional looking website, whilst being an absolute lead generating demon.

It ultimately comes down to a choice in font, colours, choice of background tones and textures, the (sensible) use of images and the style and type of buttons. Don't worry, I'm not going to get all ultra geeky on you, but if you want to know how to create the perfect website, this book will help you.

What should your website look like?

I started out in the web design field as what you could call a typical web designer. Everything I focused on, was "what it looked like", and I did focus so heavily on design that everything we produced looked great. We had great feedback from clients, in that they were very happy with how their website *looked*. I didn't have any testimonials as to how their website *performed*.

But then, my attitude to web design was simple - that your website was just something to make your business look professional. I didn't really focus on things like lead magnets, or call to actions, because quite simply - I didn't understand. Or more to the point, I didn't know.

But of course, *I didn't know*, what I didn't know.

Then over the years, as I discovered more about marketing in general, I realised that focusing on design wasn't the best thing to do. I learned that copy (i.e. the text) was more important, and readability was crucial. I found out about things like reading gravity (where basically the eye naturally reads down, and reading up goes against what you instinctively want to do, so don't put a call to action *above* crucial copy).

So taking this new information, and building on what I'd been learning, I started to build websites in a very different way. So much so, I practically removed all real styling from my own website with the view - style doesn't really matter - copy does.

But of course, despite the fact I thought I was great at writing copy - I was still pretty rubbish (by my current standards, at least). So the situation I was now in, was that my website didn't look great, and the copy still wasn't that much better anyway. As such, I struggled to win new business. People weren't converting and I didn't really understand why.

Things started to change for me around 2013/2014. This was the time I joined a mastermind group from one of the UK's biggest sources of marketing information. It was less mastermind, more information… but still, it had some value.

And in the early days of it in particular, I learnt a vast amount of stuff. I realised I needed to make a good mix of both great copy, and great design. Over the next five years we got progressively better, and better at design, whilst maintaining the direct response style.

So to reiterate, the absolute worst thing you could do is purely focus on having a pretty website, but you've got to have a good design to a degree to help you build authenticity.

More and more web designers are learning about direct response marketing, and that's great, but many will still just focus on the design. They'll focus on making you look good, but won't actually take into consideration the importance of a return on your investment. All they're bothered about is impressing you, making you feel like you've got value for money, and having something snazzy to put in their portfolio.

And I reiterate, they don't do this to deceive you (generally speaking) - they do this because they don't know what they don't know.

Now before I get in too deep talking about design in general, I'm going to tackle branding first, because branding is the one thing that most businesses religiously focus on… and I mean obsess over. Many business owners that I know are (or were once, at least) so enamoured with their branding and logo that the suggestion that adverts and landing pages should run without a logo is mind boggling.

The further suggestion, that various pages on your own website don't need to have any focus on your logo, is completely unbelievable to them. And to you too, I'm sure?

You're reading this, possibly shaking your head, saying "well, it might work for some but it wouldn't work for me".

But remember, your brand doesn't matter in itself. Branding overall, and the look and feel of your site, definitely matters in terms of making things feel complete, or perhaps feel consistent, but your actual logo is irrelevant. I can't say this enough.

The whole thing should feel well put together, and it should have a feeling of authenticity to it… but let me repeat myself (because it's so important): design and branding is important, but it's not the only thing that you should have key focus on.

Sounds like I want the best of both worlds, right?

Well, yeah, I kind of do want that.

I wrote an email out to my list the other day, because I was reviewing some of my team's work. I was stunned at one of the designs we'd just rolled out, it looked amazing. But better still, it had everything 'right'. The right headline, the right layout, the right call to action, everything was right, *and* it looked incredible.

But we've spent years - literally years and years perfecting the art. So rather than focus on making it super fancy and pretty - focus on making it functional, readable, and authentic. Keep it looking good, yes - but don't forgo great copy over great design.

As I've mentioned said a million times already, no-one, and I mean no-one - with the exception of your significant other and maybe your mum, cares about your brand. They don't care about your logo. They don't really care about your colour scheme (unless it's something garish or offensive, or makes use of bright red which is a 'warning' colour), and they certainly don't care how long you've been in business.

The latter can be useful for building credibility, but my point here is you shouldn't make that the biggest selling point, or at least, not the introductory text on your website (along with a nice big headline saying 'welcome to my website'). What you *should* focus on is: How you can help your prospective client fix their problem, or provide them the product or service that they really want?

The best way I can think of describing it is this: Let's just say that Website A and Website B have pretty much identical copy. Website A is laid out well, and the copy is readable. But there's no branding at all, even though it might have a splash of colour here and there, overall it looks boring and plain.

Website B is laid out *almost* identically, but it makes use of some good graphics and, quite simply, is far more attractive. Branding is carried through the whole site, and everything looks like it's had someone paying attention to detail.

In general, i.e. in probably over 95% of scenarios, the better looking website will win. I'm sure you don't really struggle with this concept either. It's obvious. The site that looks the most professional, and that has had the most attention to detail, will perform best.

So in general, a website (or any piece of marketing) that looks good as well as features good readability, strong copy and a call to action compared to an identical website that looks bland and uninteresting, the well designed one will work better.

That's not me just coming up with random opinion either, this is based on extensive testing and measuring we've done for ourselves as well as my clients.

Remember, direct response marketing is the process where we forget about your brand, your logo and indeed any ethos you might have, for the sole purpose of doing one thing: engaging the reader and ultimately creating a response.

So let's recap: a good, strong brand is important if you want your material to look professional and you want your prospective customer/client to feel like everything has been polished and had good attention to detail. It absolutely must not interfere with the most important rules of direct response marketing.

You should have a headline. It should be an attention grabbing headline that creates interest, enough to get the reader to read the next line of copy. And there should be lots of good, strong compelling copy with a way to take action, a reason to take action and most importantly a reason to take action now.

Your headline should be text, not an image. I've seen a lot of websites in my time, for prospective clients and the like, and you wouldn't believe (well, you probably would) how many have their logo and navigation bar, then a huge photo that's got only something vaguely to do with what they actually do.

Before I completely trash the idea, it's OK to make use of a 'hero image', (that is, an image that takes up a good 1/3 or more of the browser, normally just under the navigation/logo). However, you should only make use of an image like this where it's relevant, adds to the design, but doesn't (and I can't stress this bit enough), impact the readability of the headline text - which in this particular design style should be over the image.

But on that note, you should never have text directly over an image without something to make sure the text is readable. So if you're using a hero image, you'll want the text to be over the image but with a transparent background behind the text.

Or perhaps the image will be darkened or lightened so that the headline text in white/black will be readable. But I really can't stress enough, how it's a "nice to have" and should only be used where it reinforces one of the key points: Authenticity and overall branding.

I know it's tempting, but you shouldn't have rotating, scrolling or fading images where the text changes. Primarily for this reason: how annoying is it when the timing of the rotating image/text doesn't correlate with your text reading speed and/or loading time on your browser?

As you just get to a bit of text that interests you, the text changes.

We've all been frustrated by that at some point, I'm sure, but it's more than that.

How can you know which headline or piece of text works best?

It completely hinders your ability to test and measure the success or failure of your website copy. In the vast majority of circumstances, you shouldn't be sending traffic (and by that I mean pay per click traffic etc) to your home page. Traffic you pay to bring to your website should go to landing pages (I'll come to those in a bit).

By having a strong headline on your homepage which doesn't rotate, you can get an understanding of how well it's working for organic traffic, referrals, and maybe certain advertising where simply it's easier to just promote your homepage (although as I've said, you really want to send any traffic you can to dedicated landing pages).

Whilst we're on the subject of images, what sort of photos should you use?

How many should you use? Should they be big? Small? Should they be clickable?

So many questions about such a tiny aspect … but it's all ultra-important.

An important rule to remember is that a photo - particularly one with people in it - draws in the eye.

That might sound obvious but it's often forgotten and overlooked. The upshot of this is, if you use a photo, especially anywhere near important copy, then you must have a caption which, in an ideal world, is clickable and is a call to action. A call to action is simply what it says; it's telling the user to do something to proceed. Click here, Order now, Get a call back, etc.

Photos can be a huge distraction and can often take people's eyes away from crucial copy at the wrong time, so use them sparingly. I often find using a photo full width on the browser is good to break up parts of copy, but remember that if you're going to have text over an image you absolutely must have a background box behind the text. Never ever have plain text over an image – it's impossible to read, actually it's worse than that, because it frustrates the reader and subsequently you'll be even more likely to lose them.

As I just mentioned, I normally do something like having a black or white transparent box (which – if we're getting technical – has opacity of about 75-80%) and large black or white thick text. Obviously the colour choices are related to the type of image and website design overall. But with this sort of text, whether it's on the hero image or just later down in the design, you only want one or two lines of text maximum in this scenario – it keeps it looking good, but keeps it readable.

That means you'll probably want the text size to be 25-35pt in size. That probably wants to shrink when you get to mobile, though.

Just remember the crucial thing here is that readability is the ultimate aim.

So whilst we're on design, let's talk about that. I see website after website after website that is stupid. They have the text in such a way that it's damn near impossible for me to read it – and I have 20/20 vision and I'm not colour blind.

It's a fast way to lose business, and more than that I actually get angry at these people who implement this, especially if I was actually interested in the product/service.

Most people probably just squint, try a bit harder then give up. Either way, it's not the reaction you want.

Something my design team know all too well, is: White background, black text. I usually really only enforce this for block text, i.e. paragraphs of text in the main copy.

If you want, you could go light grey as a background, which works for things like headlines, (where the text is really big), but for normal paragraphs of text, keep it to black on white where you can.

This isn't just me opting for a dull looking bit of text, you need it this way because it's the way we've been trained to read over our entire lives. Reading books, papers, magazines, etc., everything is invariably black on white.

I will often keep text justified, and indent the first line of each paragraph. This is because of how we've been trained to read (think about books, think about this book) BUT I will say this: I make many exceptions to this rule, and that is quite simply when it looks odd, or it's simply not applicable, because it's a block of text on its own, or it's broken up with lots of white space in between.

If the design allows, you can keep the text simply justified, but if there's a lot of text, definitely indent it. It boils down to this: Use your common sense. If you look at it and it looks stupid, hard to read and/or ugly, there's a hell of a good chance that your prospects will think the same thing.

Don't go by what your web designer says is possible either, and don't go by what your web designer says they think is best. At the very least, ask for proven results justifying their recommendation. Either way, by the time you've finished reading this book you'll be fully versed in direct response marketing and that, is worth far more to you than any flashy design or image on your website – so you'll know better.

Actually I mentioned something here that I hear a lot of - that something is impossible.

Having either seen or implemented a whole bunch of crazy websites and functionality over the last decade and a bit, I can tell you there is little that's not possible.

If you want a dancing camel on your screen to start distributing pictures and text before everything swirls around the screen and displays cat pictures, it can be done.

I don't recommend it, obviously, but it can be done.

What a web designer normally means when they say "it can't be done" is "I don't want to", or probably more specifically "I don't know how to".

I had a rule when I started out doing web design, because I was a coder, not a designer – that you can do pretty much <u>anything</u>. It might require a lot of code, and therefore it might cost a lot, but if you have a crazy idea – it can come to fruition.

I *knew* that pretty much anything was possible, even ten years ago when there was next to nothing when it comes to the tools that we have now, I managed to implement some crazy awesome stuff.

That's not be bragging (well, I guess it kind of is…) but it's more me trying to demonstrate the point, that I have always had the attitude 'it can be done'. Most times these days when people come to me with crazy ideas, rather than implementing them we discuss how it's all going to work and decide to take another route, simply because it makes more sense.

Because what looks amazing on a desktop, whether it's parts of the website floating around to come together or whatever - if you bring it to a mobile it'll look rubbish. Or won't work. Or both.

And nothing frustrates people more than a website that doesn't work - especially if it's advertising a product or service they want.

When it comes to design, you can have whatever you want. However most of the time it will serve you better to focus on the readability and functionality of the website, and make sure that when someone lands on your website they understand that they're in the right place and they know the action they need to take.

So, I've talked a lot about how your website should look and feel but I haven't really talked about the nitty gritty how your website should be structured.

What pages should there be?

What software should you use?

What are landing pages and why do you need them?

So many questions, so let's crack on.

First of all, there's no 'right way' to structure your website, really. It almost entirely depends on the sort of content you've got, and that depends on what you've got on offer, alongside what action you want people to take.

Everyone should have a website that is easy to use, simple to navigate, but allows for one of the most important pieces of marketing material that could ever exist: your personality.

I'm not suggesting you use this as artistic licence to go and make it all bright colours and fluffy pictures, but the look/feel of it should mean that you're authentically conveying 'you', your personality and your business.

My favourite layout, which I tend to always enforce to a degree, has a number of points. It has these points because most websites have them. Now I've said before and I'll say again, you should not copy your competition. But you also shouldn't do things differently just to do them differently... sometimes things are the way they are because it makes sense.

And when it comes to websites, there are things that are the way they are, because we've all accessed billions of websites since the Internet first appeared, and the vast majority of them have a certain layout.

I remember at University (rather depressingly, that was many years ago now…) my web design lecturer talking us through 'mystery meat'.

This was metaphor for a website which was presented to you, and you had absolutely no idea what to do. You'd have to take the plunge and eat the mystery meat by clicking the link, or - more likely – you'd end up just getting frustrated and leaving.

Whilst I'd like to think we're long past websites like that, we still have websites produced today that make no sense to me at all. It's because there are people who want to 'stand out' and 'be different'.

I'm all for standing out, and being different. Totally into that, 110%. *But…* Navigation bars in random locations or in foreign locations to that which we're used to, scrolling bits where there shouldn't be scrolling bits, and so forth - all these things do nothing but confuse the user.

A few months ago, I was browsing competitor websites.

I was largely just curious, but it's always good to look at what your competition is doing. I know most of my 'big' local competitors and I'm familiar with their websites. They're all snazzy, full of portfolios and lots of glitter. That's all fine, and to be expected.

But for the majority of web designers I didn't recognise, their websites were terrible. And one in particular, I sat on the page for about 15 minutes trying to navigate it. I actually got angry, because I kept saying to myself "You must be doing something stupid, this can't be this hard, it's a bloody website for God's sake…".

Sadly, I wasn't mistaken, it was a website that functioned basically by having a menu of icons, so you had to guess what the icons meant.

And no, they weren't obvious.

So the secret to a good website is to keep it the same whilst being different (I'm just full of useful statements like that, aren't I?).

But my point in general is this: your navigation bar should be at the top, it's OK to use a MENU (with the three lines or similar) next to it as long as it's *obvious*. That should go in the top right, if it's replacing a navigation bar.

If you have a phone number - that should be prominent and in the top right. It should be plain text, i.e. not an image. This enables browsers on phones to pick up on the fact it's a number and allow you to push to call it.

Logos, if in use at all, should be in the top left or perhaps central, if nothing much else is going on in the header. Ultimately they should be insignificant as far as the design/layout goes, because you don't want the eye to be drawn to them.

I say this not because I want you to be boring, and conform. I say this, because this is what people expect when they come to your website, and if you deliberately do the opposite, unless you've done it really well, all you're going to do is frustrate your users.

Confession, I used to hate e-commerce. I could never get it to 'work'. Going back a decade to the first e-commerce site I was involved in, getting sales on it was enormously difficult. The main reason for this is, as I've already mentioned before, as a general rule the visitor that arrives at your website isn't ready to buy.

They're researching, thinking about it, comparing prices or options, but they're not buying. Not until *they're* ready. So you need to capture as many leads as possible, and re-market to them over and over.

Some years ago now, after I'd learnt about lead generation to a degree, I got involved with an e-commerce site. I tried to use the lead generation route, but struggled. I later realised that the reason I was struggling was that my client wasn't listening to me, and the follow up really wasn't great. That in itself is one of the reasons I really immerse myself in the whole process, a lot more now than I used to.

For example, when we're producing a website for someone, or landing pages for Google Ads perhaps, we'll write all the content. It means that everything is produced in the right style and has a far greater chance of being successful.

The thing is, if people are searching for your exact product, i.e. they've typed in a specific model number of a product – then as long as your website and checkout process is good - you'll probably do OK on Google Ads.

The great thing with Google Ads, is you can explicitly track your ROI, so I can deliver a report to my client(s) saying for example, for every £1 you spent on Google Ads last month, you earned £16.50.

One of the biggest problems with this though: Price.

While you have to be sensible about things, and not go over charging - the last thing you want to do is be price competitive; you don't want to be the lowest around and you sure as hell don't want to offer 'price guarantees'.

You might be shaking your head at this point but believe me, if you position yourself at the top of your market, you deal with only the 'high end' clientele, and you have a good lead generation and follow up strategy: Price becomes irrelevant.

It doesn't mean you can go about charging £300 for a £100 widget unless you're adding serious value. Offering things like VIP memberships for exclusive offers, free delivery and other benefits is a great way to bump up the average order value, however. Also, making sure you're offering bundles will help increase the average order value too.

The real secret to success with e-commerce though, is first of all to ensure you've done everything that we've covered so far. Tackle authenticity as an absolute fierce priority, and make sure that your whole site is secure and has an SSL Certificate. Get a good one, that turns the address bar green (they're not much, the basic ones are at *most* a few hundred £/$).

Following that, it's absolutely critical that you make lead generation and follow up work for you. One of the first ways you can start lead generation off, is to have a 'pop over' form that asks simply for nothing more than their email address in exchange for 10% off their first order. I'm picking 10% off as an arbitrary offer - you choose something that's relevant and appropriate to you but also that creates a compelling offer to your prospective customer.

Sure you'll get people cycling through email addresses to continually get the 10% discount, but not many. It'll be negligible.

But really, who cares? They're still ordering, but if they're cycling through email addresses it's because they know you, i.e. they're not likely to be coming back to you via Pay Per Click so in terms of your 'cost of sale' it's not much to give away.

This should help you start building your list; and on top of the 10% discount you could have a sequence of 10 or 20 emails where you're introducing yourself, your company and your products. Then you regularly email (I suggest daily, but I'll cover this more in the follow up section) with follow up offers and promotions.

This works well for e-commerce but works outstandingly for takeaways. Having had some experience first-hand of this in the past, I would get great results from a relatively small list (just a few thousand) which was continually growing.

Depending on the sort of products you're selling, you might

have a large amount of repeat purchases. In this scenario, you should find that you'll have a top 20% of your customers, i.e. people that will buy regularly and buy the more expensive products.

Segmenting your list and making sure you market more to those people would be a very, very wise thing indeed. If you're not familiar with the 80/20 rule, go read the 80/20 Principle by Richard Koch. Once you've identified the top 20%, why not reward them? Give them VIP delivery rates/times or bonus products.

There are stacks of ideas for ways to improve e-commerce response rates, but I'd focus on the essentials. Authenticity first, then get your basic lead generation up and running

Landing Pages

I'm often asked about Landing Pages and how to get the most out of them. It's a really important part of lead generation. Now the great thing about landing pages is they can apply to any business. E-commerce, Business To Business, Business To Consumer, it doesn't matter.

I've mentioned landing pages a little already, but as we're going to talk about this in depth let's really be absolutely clear what a landing page is.

In the most simple definition I can think of - the landing page is the page where someone 'lands' on your website when they click on an advert.

So you run an ad in Google, or Facebook or wherever. Someone clicks on that ad, and they come to your website. The page they're now looking at is your landing page.

Generally speaking, you can't get to the landing page from within your website. If you're browsing your website and you have a typical 5 page site, you might have Home, About, Services, Testimonials and Contact Us. Behind the scenes however, you might have 200 landing pages all for different adverts within your Pay Per Click campaigns.

Sometimes you may want to 'think outside the box' a little, and I mention E-commerce for a specific reason. We've already discussed why conversion rates are so low on E-commerce websites - most people just aren't in the position to buy.

There's no real logic to it either, I often know I want buy certain things, I'm just not in the mood to buy.

And that's something you've got to get into your mind - that you can't control when people want to buy. You can influence, and you can assist, but you can't *control*.

And it's not just buying either. Several times I've seen things that really interest me, but need me to opt-in. However I'm not always in the mood or position to opt in – maybe I've just arrived at the train station and I've got to hop off and get to work (this actually happened the other day, I saw something and was about to opt in just as I arrived at my stop).

So what's the best way to deal with this? Do we just have to put up with the fact that we're losing loads of leads and sales and there's nothing we can do about it?

The simple answer is, when we're bringing traffic to our landing pages we make an assumption. We assume they don't want to buy, or enquire. We make it easy for them to buy or enquire, obviously, but we assume that they're researching.

And if they're researching, what are they going to want? More information. The best way to offer that information? Well, that's down to you. A guide, PDF, something through the post, email series, whatever.

That's your lead magnet, and I'll cover that more extensively in the next section. But let's just cover how we're going to convince someone to opt-in in the first place.

I've already mentioned authenticity. It's extremely hard to get a landing page looking basic enough to reduce distraction, but authentic enough to build the trust. Given how important authenticity is, how can you make a page look authentic but remove distractions?

This is really where the landing page builders come into play. As a web developer at heart, I always want to code things up manually. It's taken me years to drag myself away from the development software and stop myself getting involved.

But with the variety of tools out there, you can build attractive landing pages that are entirely content focused with ease.

It *is* possible to get a landing page with just text to work, but I think one with images works better. I know I've done nothing but bang on about how brand isn't really important, and how the copy is the most important part of any landing page, and that's a valid point – but if it looks *too* basic, you'll often lose that initial credibility you need to inspire the confidence for the user to click 'get a call back'.

There are really two main types of landing page: Long copy and short copy. Long copy pages are my favourite, because you can often generate all the necessary calls to action etc. within the 'above the fold' section. It's not always easy, but it should be a priority.

Then there's the unforgivable sin: Allowing the page to have an unclear purpose (especially above the fold). What I mean by that, is that it should be absolutely crystal clear that the visitor is on the right page and what you want their next action to be (i.e. scroll to read on, click, etc).

Remember that bulk text should be black text on a white background, but I'll often intersperse sections with a splash of colour and some big white text with a quote, testimonial, or similar. It helps break up the page a bit, and makes it look good, it's a win/win in terms of building the overall look/feel of the page.

Finally, the most important thing is to have relevant links to relevant pages but make sure they're the hell out of the way of the main flow of reading. You want to link to things like a Privacy Policy and the Homepage as standard – but you might want to create similarly themed/related landing pages, and link to those slightly more obviously. The main thing is always have a strong call to action.

I'm going to deviate away from landing pages just for a moment, but you'll see why, and you'll see how it all comes back together.

Now we're all used to seeing Ads on Facebook; it's one of the things they've managed to implement really well now. It's part of your news feed, and most people don't even realise it. I won't often think of the stuff I see in my news feed as an advert, more as 'suggested content' - which is actually what it is - it's just someone is paying for it to be suggested.

It all comes down to targeting - and if the targeting is right, it works well because both parties get what they want (i.e. The party who wants something gets the something, and the party who's selling the something gets some dosh).

So some time ago I saw an Ad for some dog food. I'm always running out of dog food - it's a real problem for me. So the headline "Never run out of dog food again" was particularly catching.

I clicked through and this very nicely implemented landing page (note: landing page) explained to me how, if I pay just £x (I think it was something like £20) a month, I can have dog food delivered to me regularly.

They calculate how much I feed the dog based on his

age/weight/etc, and subsequently know when to send the next batch of food. And the winning deal - the first 6 weeks of food was just £1 including the 'scoop' that gave you exactly the right portion size.

Not only did this seem like a steal, but I had buckets of respect for the company for doing it. They were proving that what they had was awesome, and they knew that the majority of the customers who bought it for £1 would continue their subscription.

Yes, you'll have some who will simply cancel immediately, taking the £1 worth of food, abusing the system, but you'll always get that. However if you got 100 Customers, and even 80 of them cancelled, as long as that 20 that remained and were profitable enough to pay for sending out that first batch (say, within the first year?) then you'd do that all day long.

The second instance was for coffee.

I saw a headline, "The Smell Alone Is Ridiculous", with a picture of some coffee. Being a coffee drinker, it naturally grabbed my attention (as intended, I'm sure). I went through to another landing page, which was really well designed and carefully guided me through how to get my first batch of coffee for, you guessed it, £1.

As soon as I saw that, I thought I had to trial the experience.

So I went through and purchased some coffee.

What I really liked about this was, that they almost forced you to choose - do you want coffee every 1 week or 2 weeks?

This meant that the people that completed the transaction had agreed to get coffee on a regular basis. Now I liked this, but it was too frequent for me at the time. Since I signed up (quite some time ago now) they've changed this so you can in fact order it to arrive in pretty much any timescale. From every day to every 30 or 60 days and everything in between. This is really pretty smart.

The third experience, and I was almost looking out for these sorts of Ads now, was for shaving.

I don't quite recall the exact headline, but I think it was along the lines of "Do you shave? Never run out of toiletries again".

It could have been better, being that they pretty much only supplied razors (well, and the shaving gel etc, but it's the razors that would catch most people's eye).

Anyway, I clicked through to this awesome landing page that had this particularly swish looking razor with some initials engraved on it. Who wouldn't want their initials engraved on their razor?!

Going through the order process, I was able to get £10 off my first delivery of both the razor handle and enough blades to last 6 weeks. I think it cost £10 for me to get started, but again based on "how often do you shave" they then knew when to send me the next batch.

The fourth example is for a company selling bacon. As a serious bacon lover, this was music to my ears. They'd send me bacon every week, and thanks to an affiliate scheme they got me into, I'm getting lots of free bacon too. This makes me want to refer them even more, which works wonders for them, I'm sure.

It all started with a landing page which I clicked through to from Facebook and read all about them, their company and their ethos. The first pack was something like £2 instead of £4.95 and I thought, what the hell?! Why not?!

The fifth and final example is another 'meat' company - an online butchers.

Now I'm really fussy about where I get meat from, I want to make sure it's free range and humanely treated and slaughtered. The landing page I clicked through to explained a lot of this, and gave me an offer I couldn't refuse - lots of steak at a one-time discounted price.

The thing is, in all five of the above scenarios I have paid all of them quite a bit of money, but I only really buy from a couple now. My bacon by post is something I never want to live without, but I only run it for a little bit every now and then. Look at what I order in an annual basis and work out my "lifetime value" to them, and they don't do bad out of me. But I don't run it weekly (I'd often find circumstances just meant I was accumulating bacon).

Then there's the dog food. They claimed, as I recall, each batch was "custom made" to meet the requirements of your dog. But our dog required a lower protein diet and despite each batch being 'custom made' they couldn't tweak that recipe.

As a result, our dog didn't get on with it (the smell from his backside was horrendous) and we eventually phased it out and went back to his usual brand. That was with Andy, my last dog, and he always had a sensitive stomach anyway. I re-subscribed when we got Ralph - and he got on with it fine, but then we hired a dog trainer. She recommended a particular type of food and organised everything for us, so in fairness to them - I don't think there's any way they could have retained me.

Next, let's take the coffee; I cancelled originally because I could only have it delivered every 1 or 2 weeks, I believe. It was more than what we were drinking, and as much as I enjoyed making coffee it was an effort.

Then a while back I got an Espresso Machine and my life changed - I could pour beans in at the top, press a button and it'd do it all. Bliss. Remembering they did really good coffee, I signed back up and I've been with them for as long as I can remember now.

Then we have the shaving company - there's nothing they could have done to keep me.

Firstly, I just didn't get on with the razor in the long term (it wasn't as good as the leading 'big brand' razor) but secondly and more to the point - I've adopted a 'stubbly' look over the last couple of years.

Finally - the butchers; the meat quality was inconsistent and I had a lot of problems with them. After one important order came completely wrong (important because I was cooking for people) I got annoyed, but gave them the benefit of the doubt.

The final straw was some meat coming to me that was obviously not entirely fresh, because it smelled mildly off on receipt; after a couple of days it was inedible.

Now one final point before I return to landing pages, in all five of these scenarios, payment was extremely easy and I had to do nothing special to get the recurring payments working - meaning unless I actually went in and cancelled, they'd just assume I wanted more stuff and they would charge me more money.

The point I want to stress, and the whole reason behind this whole big long story, is that a decision was made on the landing page.

In all five of the above scenarios, I either bought there and then, *or* opted in to more marketing where I was then continually reminded about the product and given a link to return back to them. I did also 'save' the links in Facebook a few times but the point is, each page was well written, well designed, and gained my trust.

The landing pages for your marketing are so ridiculously important, I cannot stress it enough. It will be the deciding factor as to whether your campaign is a success, or a failure.

I'll finish this section with sales copy; this tends to be the biggest let down with landing pages and even my own have suffered with 'poor' sales copy.

Remember that the sales copy you produce for landing pages needs to be concise and focus on the specific needs of that 'search' (or to be cohesive with your advert on social media). This is why we want multiple versions of landing pages to encourage the call to action.

If someone has searched for "problems with X" you want to take people to a page about X. Not a generic page, not a page talking about X, Y and Z – but a page talking about X.

In terms of writing the copy itself, remember that you should focus on the basics. Focus on their pain, and how you can help them out of pain with your product and/or service.

Write using the rules AIDA – Attention, Interest, Decision and Action, and make sure when you're getting onto the Action, make the button obvious and clickable.

That reminds me of one final point – when you're building your landing page, don't have a million buttons visible on the screen at any one point.

I always say how critical it is to have buttons visible on the page at any one point, but I saw one the other day where there were three buttons visible on the page at the same point - and they really didn't need to be. One would have sufficed, possibly two at the absolute outside.

The one approach I always use when it comes to looking at a landing page and verifying both the authenticity and sales copy, is to close it down, close my eyes – take a moment... reopen it and pretend I'm viewing that page for the first time

Try it.

Put yourself in your prospect's shoes.

Would You fill out the form?

Would You take action?

Once you're comfortable with that answer, you're ready to rock and ready to send some traffic to it. Remember, test and measure! Run traffic to that page for a little while, see what the conversion rate is like, make some changes and repeat. Keep going and keep doing variations until you've got the conversion rates as good as you can get!

You often see long and short landing pages and you're probably wondering, which works best? It's a good question and you're going to hate my answer.

Quite simply there is no right or wrong answer.

I could say something like "long copy always outperforms short copy" but the problem with that is, I'm not omnipotent and I can't see all the results for all the landing pages and sales letters in the whole world.

But what I can say is, that from experience of what we've dealt with in the past, we've had some great results from long copy pages *and* short copy pages alike, but it all completely and utterly depends on the 'sale'. By that, I mean it depends on what action you're asking people to take. Is it opt-in to more marketing? Is it to put their hand in their pocket? And if so, is it a lot of money?

If it's just to opt-in and it's just say, name and email, you could probably get away with a really short copy page. In some ways that might outperform a long copy page, because people just need 30 seconds (or less) on the page before deciding to opt in.

But if you're asking them to put their hand in their pocket, even for just a few £/$/€ you've got bigger issues at hand - you've got to build something I've already gone on about a fair bit - trust.

Trust is hard to build online, and it normally takes a substantial / comprehensive website to convince people to put their hand in their pocket.

People are (rightly) paranoid about handing over their credit card details, so you need to make sure you've got a secure web page, and that there's plenty of sales copy and links for them to follow/check you out if they're concerned.

And that trust is enormously difficult to build on a short copy page. So, short copy or long copy? Depends.

It depends on your target market, depends on your product

and/or service but most importantly it depends on what you're offering and what you're asking for.

The more you ask for, the more you'll need to build trust. Personally, I think the best way to approach this is to have a good quality, medium length landing page to obtain the 'opt in' details.

Then on the subsequent 'thank you' page, you make it a longer copy sales page selling whatever it is you want as your 'wallet opener'. For example, for me, that might be this book. It might be a course. Either way it's something low value in terms of money, but it should deliver high in terms of value for the recipient. This book only costs £30, but the potential value of it is immeasurable, because it's proportionate to your company earnings etc.

Following on from that, I would then make the higher end 'offer' which is ultimately, the main product or service you want to sell.

Lead Magnets

OK, so I've covered this in and out a little already, but let's talk lead magnets. So what exactly is a lead magnet? Quite simply it's something you can use to encourage prospects to turn into leads. They volunteer information in exchange for the lead magnet. Up to now I've almost exclusively used my book as my lead magnet – but I've started to expand with some additional resources recently, including this one. This very thing you're reading right now is my lead magnet.

Your lead magnet should revolve around your expertise, after all, there's no good in producing some knock off crap for the sake of trying to get someone's details. If your lead magnet is poor quality, you'll be poor quality by association.

Now the sad fact is, the majority of people who sign up for PDFs and similar lead magnets never read them. It's not because they don't want to, but think about it … how often have you signed up for something and sat waiting for it in your inbox, only to get bored because it's not instant so then you go do something else?

But also, sometimes opening your email can be effort. If I choose to use a personal email account (because it's personal, or because I'm using one of my more junky email addresses as it's a source I don't trust) then I've got to open a browser, type in the relevant URL for outlook.com or gmail.com – then login.

Effort.

It's not much effort, but it's some effort… and subsequently it's only going to happen if I actually really want to read the resource right there and then. Sometimes I think I'll sign up for it and read it later… only later never comes.

This is why follow up is so crucial (covered in the next section) but regardless, you need to give your lead a couple of chances at reading / viewing the resource.

I signed up to something recently that I thought "I'd like to check that out but not right now". I liked the person I signed up with because they gave me a good few chances to get what I'd signed up to, despite not actually taking action.

All of this is to labour the point that you've got to make it easy to get to your lead magnet. You've got to assume they get distracted whilst reading/viewing your lead magnet, and you've got to make sure your lead magnet is of high enough quality that if you signed up for it yourself you'd be impressed.

If you're sitting here wondering what the hell you can write, don't worry, it's easy. You know your trade, right? Whatever it is you do, whatever it is you sell, you must undoubtedly talk to your prospects at some point. You get asked questions about your product or service.

Typical questions, no doubt … but questions nonetheless. Queries about the product, service or even industry are not uncommon.

All you've got to do to start writing your lead magnet is write down five questions you think are the most valuable to your prospects. Then, in each of the questions, write just one line (or more if you can) answering that question.

When you've answered all five, go back over it and try to expand the sentence into maybe two, or three sentences – so that you've build up your first paragraph.

Then once you're done going over it a second time, go back over it again and try to expand out each answer into just two paragraphs. Once you've done that, repeat.

You should be able, without much effort at all, to get to a good 3-4 paragraphs on each question. Hopefully you're onto at least a side of A4.

Now as long as the answers are useful and a bit more than 'common sense' – you've got yourself a good lead magnet. Some can be short, some can be long – the ultimate goal is value.

The next issue that's an important issue with a lead magnet, is the format of it.

Should it be designed? Should it be in PDF format? How do you deliver it? All good questions and all shall be answered.

Well, let me take 'should it be designed?' first, because this is an important question for many. In fact, it puts off people from doing their own lead magnet because they think they're not capable.

Should it be more than just a word document? Yes of course … but does it take much effort? Not really.

The ones that we design look really good, and professional, but that's to be expected. We have a graphic designer creating them.

Am I a graphic designer? No. Did I have reasonable looking

lead magnets before hiring a graphic designer? Yes.

All it takes is a simple image here and there, that's relevant to the text you're talking about. First of all, structure it like it's a guide. That is to say, put a front page on it with a title – and your name. Make it clear it's something you have produced.

Second, let's just say you've broken your guide into five points. Find yourself five images (either from a stock photo site or worst case, use Google Images - but make sure you select the options that brings up images for commercial use). I'd then simply put each image alongside each point.

Perhaps create a 'back page' which is just a quick write up on you, with a photo of you, and contact details and a call to action.

The whole thing might only be 4 or 5 pages long, but as long as the information in it is useful, you've got a great lead magnet.

The next question you may have, is what 'format' should it be in. Word? PDF?

Well, my recommendation would be PDF – and in the modern versions of Word you can simply 'save as' PDF (it's in the drop down of formats which defaults to 'Word Document').

So the final question then, is how do you deliver it? This is a trickier question to answer, because it largely depends on what email marketing platform and what website software you're using.

Traditionally, I would email a link to the guide, rather than attaching it. So you can upload it to your website simply as a file, then link to it that way.

Sure, people can just send a link of that to other people, or share it online … but most of the time that's not really a big deal.

It's not a big deal because most of your leads won't even think to do that, they'll simply refer to the landing page in the first place. While I do appreciate that you might get very paranoid and want to 'protect' your content from being plagiarised or 'stolen'

– nine times out of ten, people will find a way no matter what you do.

You can spend endless hours (or even days) worrying about how to 'protect' your lead magnet or other resources, but my advice is to simply worry more about how easy it is to get it in the first place. If you make it ridiculously easy and fast for people to download simply by putting in their email, then they'll put in their email.

If people are going to go to lengths to 'steal' your resources, well, they're not going to be good customers for you in the long run are they? So they're nothing to worry about.

To summarise, you should create a guide filled with useful content and make it look as good as you can. Then, save it as PDF and upload it to your website, so that you email out a link as part of your email sequence. Simple enough, right?

Chapter Four:
Getting Found

These days, when people ask you about your marketing, especially online marketing, the first thought is almost always either Google, or Facebook. They're the two biggest players in generating traffic for sure, but when it comes to getting eyeballs on your landing pages, it's a bit more complicated than just "running some ads" on Facebook or Google.

That being said, I'm going to be totally up front and say, this is one of my favourite subjects - mainly because one of the prime ways of getting found *is* Google Ads, and *that's* one of my favourite things because it connects people who are *searching* for a specific thing *with* a specific thing.

Well, usually, anyway… if it's done right.

All too frequently (and this is what Google work so hard to eradicate) you'll search for something and the results will be irrelevant at best, or completely obscure at worst.

So let's get started… I want to cover the most obvious ways of getting found. First you have search engines. I think, unless you've been living under a rock for the last 15 years, you'll know what a search engine is. It's a website, which allows you to search for things. Google is by far the biggest and the main search engine that people use, although Bing is also heavily used (and even more so in the USA).

When it comes to search engines, the tendency by many people is to go for "organic" listings. You've no doubt heard the term Search Engine Optimisation (SEO). Well, I'll talk about it briefly, but probably won't be telling you what you want to hear. I know I've upset a few clients and potential clients (and lost sales) because of my views on this, but I know I'm right.

I'm right because I've seen tiny companies and huge companies tackle SEO and I've seen companies of all sizes fail. And not just fail in SEO, I've seen companies fail *because* of SEO. If you're reliant on Google organic (or Pay Per Click, or *any one platform* for that matter), then you need to change how you work and change fast. Being reliant on just one platform is dangerous. Doing it *knowingly* is asking for trouble.

I've seen companies invest £1000's and even £10,000's <u>per</u> <u>month</u> into SEO, to get to a great position, but then as soon as they stop paying (or even in a couple of cases whilst they were *still* paying) their position drops. Dramatically.

An algorithm change or tweak, or simply someone like Google deciding they don't like *you* any more, there's nothing you can do about it. So simply, SEO is stupid for the following two reasons: one, you <u>can't</u> control it or rely on it, and two you <u>can't</u> scale it.

You might think you can control it, but you can't. You're ultimately trying to trick Google into pushing you higher up the ranks than Google thinks you deserve to be.

That's all you're doing, whether you like it or not. You can whack loads of content on your site if you want to be a relevant information source, but are you really going to get buyers from that? Probably not. Copy written for search engines does not make good copy for humans. You want copy that creates desire and interest, not packed with a gazillion keywords around the subject you're trying to boost.

And then there's scaling it. Scaling something is crucial to business success, and if you manage to get some good results from SEO from investing £50k, and you get to the best you possibly can get, *then what*? With Pay Per Click (PPC) you can continually increase spending to continually get more back.

The one disclaimer I will put here is, my sentiments here apply to the 'average business'. By that I mean a business of £0 to perhaps £1m. If you're at a point where your budgets exceed the spend available, i.e. if you've got more money available than there's traffic to buy, then *of course* you should look at things like SEO... but it should be done in a very particular way. My comments just a few moments ago still apply: a page designed to please a search engine is not necessarily a page designed to please a prospective client.

After search engines, we then have display advertising (think, banner adverts, Facebook ads, LinkedIn ads and much more).

The sad fact of the matter is, though, that most business owners don't really do any of the above *at all*, and even if they do they most likely don't do it properly. And that's made worse by the fact they'll probably happily spend £1000's if not £10,000's on their website!

I reviewed some ads in a magazine a while back, and noticed that a good 30-40% of them had no websites mentioned at all. That's foolish, unless you have only one specific call to action you want people to follow – but in the case of the ones I reviewed I think they simply didn't think to put their website on.

It's extra foolish because, if you're advertising in somewhere like a magazine, and you manage to get someone to even just glance at your website, you have the opportunity to have 're-marketing' to them later. How that works is another subject in itself, but it works on the same principle I'm sure you're familiar with: You go look at shoes on a website, then you get nothing but ads for shoes everywhere.

But this is seriously useful, because in the case that they saw your ad in a magazine, took one look online but then got distracted or whatever – for the foreseeable future you're able to advertise to them online.

Pretty cool, I think.

Although I will say it's "not cool" to suddenly spam then with adverts… that's not what it's about. It's simply about reminding them about your product/service so they can enquire/buy when they're ready.

Additionally, you don't know *when* people are reading the

paper/magazine, and there's a good chance they're reading at a time convenient to them – not you. Subsequently, they might not be in the position to pick up the phone to you, or you might not be open and they can't phone you.

So a web-based call to action is one of the safest, and most convenient, as long as it's easy to get to (don't have long, stupid, complicated URL's – if your domain name is huge, get a shorter one just for the campaign).

We've done this time and again for ourselves and our clients; made specific domains for specific adverts, simply so that it's easy and memorable for someone to find you. It can redirect to a main page on your website, but the domain in the first place should be super easy to remember.

Before I delve into the platforms in a bit more depth, one of the keys to success you'll have with Pay Per Click, is to lose the strong focus on Cost Per Click (CPC).

The CPC is normally what most people focus on, and it's the biggest roadblock to people not taking up Google Ads in the first place. And this is, unfortunately, seriously misguided.

OK, that might be a little harsh, but too many times I've dealt with say, a plumber, who won't pay £5 per click to run Ads for people looking for a boiler install. It doesn't matter what it is per click, because it's much better to look at what it is per *lead* (or even better per sale). This is referred to as Cost Per Action or Cost Per Acquisition (CPA).

And it's CPA that we really focus on.

Because it's CPA that determines whether you're going to be profitable or not.

Let's take the boiler example.

Overall cost of job: £3000

Cost of boiler/parts: £2000

Cost of labour: £500

Profit: £500

If it took 200 clicks to get 5 leads, and one of those to go ahead, you'd be down by £500.

If it took 100 clicks to get 5 leads, and one of those to go ahead, you'd be breaking even.

If it took 50 clicks to get 5 leads, and one of those to go ahead, you'd be £250 ahead.

These figures are pretty crude, but they represent the overall approach we need to take with PPC. That the CPA should be less than or equal to the profit of the job.

"Surely it should be less than the profit of the job" I hear you shout.

We're just talking about simply acquiring customers here. With Pay Per Click the most successful businesses are those that engineer repeat business over and over, or that work hard to generate referrals.

If you can start with figures close to breaking even within the first few months, then you're likely to do very well if you persist and keep improving your campaigns. Remember, and burn the phrase into your head, "It's a marathon, not a sprint".

The success to Google Ads, Facebook and any campaign - really - is constant refinement.

One last thing before I get into the platforms: On some level, you're going to want to target geographically. This might be local, or national, or targeting specific countries… but you'll need to target *some* geographic area. But maybe you're targeting geographic location because you're a bricks and mortar business looking for local people, *or* it can simply be used where your budget might be a bit limited.

Let's explain that. Say you have a limited budget and you're targeting people who are looking to sell their property anywhere in the UK. Your budget will be used up much quicker if it's a campaign targeting the whole of the UK, rather than say, Essex. This is pretty straight forward, and comes down to the number of people searching in Essex which is going to be far less than the whole of the UK. So by targeting only people in Essex we significantly reduce the number of people who may see and subsequently click on the Ad.

Even if you are a national company, it can still be worth running local campaigns. The reason for doing so is, it allows you to more easily track statistics and trends of conversion rates, as you might find that people in the South East convert to more paying Clients than people in the North West. This can be very useful if you're spending significant amounts of money in generating your leads.

Google Ads

If you've not got involved in Pay Per Click (PPC) and especially Google Ads before, the best thing to do is sign up for an account. You need to experience the interface, even if you don't actually end up running it yourself, you need to see it.

You might be worried you're not "technical enough" - but it really is quite simple. Google have made it that way on purpose (they want anyone/everyone to be able to sign up for it). If you're really clueless on where to start - head over to www.dbobible.co.uk and grab some free resources, I have a little guide on Google Ads there.

Now when it comes to 'search' Pay Per Click - your choice is really either Google or Bing. I would, if you're just starting out, focus on Google initially. Bing is great, and the system is almost identical to an "old Google", but I would only move to Bing once you're running at "max budget" on Google. That is to say, when you're bidding for all the keywords you want with a virtually unlimited daily budget.

Once you've signed up you'll need to create a campaign. The way Google have changed this over the last year or so (at time of writing, which is 2019) has made it really quite simple to plan out your campaign. You can set your targets/goals quite clearly, and it should be quite straight forward.

One thing I'll mention is (and I'll only touch on this, because platforms like Google change so often, by the time you're reading this it could have changed five times already) keep your 'search' and 'display' totally separate. If you follow the default 'wizard' for creating a campaign, you'll end up with search and display merged together and I have an issue with this for one reason.

That reason is simple. Search and display are totally different things, and you need your campaigns, ad groups and landing pages to be as specific as possible. The way you talk to people, and treat people differs massively (in my opinion) when you compare someone *searching* for something (i.e. your widget/service) and if you're *interrupting* their daily life to show them an advert for your widget/service.

The thing is, you get something like Google Ads working well for you, and it's one of the best forms of Pay Per Click because it scales well. You can literally control the flow of leads like a tap, turning it up and down with the budget.

But before I get going too deeply into Google, I need to talk to you about the first rule of pay per click. It's enormously tempting to just say "The first rule of pay per click is *you don't talk about pay per click*" but as I realise I'm getting older, and older, I realise there's a whole generation of people that wouldn't get that reference. Oh well...

So what is the first rule of Pay Per Click? Well, it's this...

The first rule of Pay Per Click is that you absolutely must not, under pretty much any circumstances, ever send people to your homepage.

When running any form of Pay Per Click or in fact, any direct response marketing campaign, you should always send people to a dedicated landing page. I've talked about landing pages already so I'm not going to repeat myself, but when it comes to Google - and Google Search especially - you will need a lot of landing pages.

The reason for this is simple.

It's to make the landing pages as specific to the search terms as possible, so that [a] the person who's searching decides they're in the right place, and [b] so that Google also knows that sending people to this page is a good thing, because it's relevant to what they're looking for.

As with many other platforms, Google has a significantly higher number of people using it than ever before, so it's actually a lot harder to 'make it work'.

Does this make it something to avoid doing?

Does it make it pointless trying to get a Return On Investment (ROI)?

Of course not.

It just means it's not easy.

Although to be fair, if I'm honest I don't think I've ever seen it be *'easy'* with Google Ads (although some industries are easier than others). But like I say, just because it's hard doesn't mean it's not worth doing. Many of our clients have been working with us for years, but in the early days it was a negative ROI and looked very challenging.

So what are the 'secrets' to success when it comes to Google? What did we do with these accounts to turn them around? How do we make it work where so many others fail? Well of course, as ever it's not just one thing. It's a lot of things.

With Google Ads specifically, it's making sure that you're 'playing the game'. Both Google and Facebook have had to really tighten up their policy/rules over the last few years, and this is, if I'm honest, your first battle.

It's very tempting to just tell them to completely ignore the policies, write up a landing page how you see fit, and run some ads. The trouble is, you can get suspended in seconds, and it can take days if not weeks or more to get back online.

So how to avoid being struck down by the policy team?

Well the first thing is, as I've already mentioned, to 'play the game'. Use the guidelines and tools in Google to help you, and you need to make sure you have a link going to a privacy policy on all pages on your website.

You've got to have a privacy policy, but you also need to qualify a few things … For example you can't make any claim about improving someone's life, health, fitness or business without qualifying that statement. For example:

"Grow your business fast and increase your profits by 100% within 12 months".

Nope. If you think you can get away with that, you need to think again. You simply can't. "But that's not fair, Ben, loads of other people make that claim and get away with it". Yeah, they may do, but they're unlikely to be able to get away with that forever.

So the thing is, there's nothing wrong with that statement if you qualify it there and then. Whilst this looks really stupid if you actually don't change the phrasing, there are ways around it. For example:

"Grow your business fast (results may vary) and increase your profits by 100% (results may vary) within 12 months (timeline may vary)"

Yeah ok that looks stupid, but that's what Google want and they want it not because they don't believe you but because they *can't* believe you.

They know nothing about you and they know nothing about what you can achieve for people, and ultimately if they allow you to say something that's not true then not only are you liable to be sued, but so are Google.

Think about it from this perspective - *you* know you're telling the truth and *you* know that you're an honest person, but there are millions of people out there who *aren't* honest and are ready to screw over the next person they find. Yeah... This is why we can't have nice things.

So a nice easy way around it is to fiddle with the wording a bit. Be a bit creative and, sure, this takes a bit more time but like I said, Google isn't as easy as it used to be.

"Grow your business fast by implementing these top tips which will help to increase your profits by up to 100% within 12 months (although obviously your results may vary)"

OK it's still not the best, and I've spent all of 15 seconds thinking up that headline – but you get my point, right? Don't make a claim without some form of disclaimer *or* a link to a third party corroborating your claim. These cannot just be testimonials; this has to be almost scientific proof – so not always easy but hey – did I say it was going to be easy?

The other ways to make Google work better for you are to use the extensions they provide. This is something almost everyone

I've worked with overlook. Google have for a long time now, prioritised those that use multiple Ad extensions over those that don't. That is to say, if all other factors are equal, the advert using more Ad extensions will be shown first.

What's that? Google are discriminating against users who don't know how to use the platform properly? They sure as hell are. But it's their platform, their rules. Like it or lump it. So ultimately, you need to make sure you're using Location extensions, Call extensions, Snippets, Call outs, the works.

The more Ad extensions you use, the higher your ranking will be at the lower cost per click. And we know what that means? That means more clicks for your budget, and that means more conversions.

Diving a little further into getting lower priced clicks, you should pay attention to your quality score for each keyword. The quality score is determined by a large number of factors. It's not just about the ad text - other considerations range from (as I've mentioned) ad extensions, to the quality of the landing page, and many other factors (many of which I'm sure we'll never know, unless we work for Google).

So whilst the Ad text is important, and you need to use as many Ad Extensions as possible, it's critical to make sure that the relevance of their search query is carried on to the page which they land on when they click your link (the landing page).

There's absolutely no point showing the customer your homepage of all sorts of ceramic items, when they've searched for 'ceramic teapots'.

Take them to a page full of ceramic teapots!

Your conversion ratio is guaranteed to be higher, but also Google will pick up on the fact that the landing page is more relevant, and subsequently your quality score will be higher.

Now focusing on Google Search is great, but you're missing out on an absolutely huge opportunity if you don't focus on a well delivered Display Advertising campaign. Why?

Well, look at it this way: How much of your day do you actually spend searching? Most of your average day will be taken up with your day to day activities or casual surfing.

What does this mean?

It means that for the vast majority of the time, every single customer you could ever want is targetable using one of these three display advertising platforms.

You might say "Banner adverts? Oh I don't click on those…"

Well, OK. You might not click on those for 99.99% of your browsing usage, but if you looked at your history over the last year, is it possible that in that 0.01% of time you might have clicked on a banner/display advertisement that caught your interest?

I didn't pick 0.01% at random – it's a common CTR (Click Through Rate) for display advertising. Between 0.01% and 0.03%.

Why bother with such a tiny percentage?

Because of the amount of impressions (people who have the opportunity to see your ad).

Think about it. If 1,000,000 people could view your ad over the course of 1 week, with a CTR of 0.01% you could have 10,000 clicks.

The CPC (Cost Per Click) tends to be lower, so you're not paying the same as someone searching for something, but that's equally reflected in the number of conversions – it will tend to be much lower with display advertising. Once you're doing everything in this book, you'll find that your conversions increase anyway, so you really can't lose.

So now we've established that Display Advertising is worth doing, how can we do it and how can we get the most out of it?

Targeting.

With all the display platforms, you get the incredible ability to pick and choose who your adverts are going to be displayed to.

Imagine that, 15 years ago someone said, "Yes, you can have an advert in my paper. It's read by 100,000 people but I can guarantee you that only men, aged 30-40 who live in this certain postcode and who happen to like golf, will read it".

It would have seemed like an impossible dream, but between Facebook, LinkedIn and Google Display Advertising, you have all of those options and more.

Google Display: Traditional Profiling

The traditional profiling route means you can select potential viewers of a certain age, by their interests, by what sort of site the banner will display on, and a whole host of other options.

I recommend you take a look at the options in as much detail as possible, and consider your target market. It will be critical to making this a success.

You want the sites the ads are displayed on to be relevant, you want the viewers interests to be in the right field for what you're selling / promoting, and as usual you can specify by gender or age.

Remember, these are approximations, it's not the accuracy Facebook or LinkedIn will give you, as the majority of Facebook/LinkedIn targeting is built up on their actual profile – but it's still pretty accurate.

Re-Marketing

Re-marketing is huge. We've all seen it, right? You've been looking at a new set of pots & pans on Amazon, and then an hour later the same pots & pans are advertised to you on Facebook.

It's amazingly powerful. It works whereby the user visits your web page, a cookie is placed on their PC, and then as they browse around other sites your advert can be displayed, because you know they've seen your site.

There are re-marketing options for Google and Facebook, I'll come back to Facebook, but for Google it's really easy to set up.

Again, because things change, I don't want to do a step by step (Google Support will help you with that) - but in a nutshell, when logged into AdWords in your Campaigns you should find something called Shared Library.

Click in to 'Audiences' and click 'New' then 'Remarketing list'. The settings after that are relatively straight forward, a name of the list, membership duration (can be up to 540 days!) and a description.

You also have 'Who to add to your list'. You can select "Visitors of a page" or "Visitors of a page with a specific tag".

The 'tag' allows you to track certain conversions (or lack of – which can be very useful for tracking abandoned carts, for example, if they got all the way to the credit card bit, then stopped).

So if you're really clever (and we do this) you can take people back to the exact same point they were at, and simply get them to complete the sale.

The tag is simply a bit of JavaScript code – if you don't manage your website just send it to your web designer and they can put it in for you.

Bing

This section will be very short, because there's not a great deal to say over Google Ads. The Bing platform looks and feels like the old Google Ads platform, although it's got its own nuances and features, it's basically the same.

The main thing to focus on is ultimately, if you do everything right on Google Ads, you won't go wrong on Bing.

Bing seems to have an older demographic of users and actually, that makes sense. Think about it from this angle, Bing is the 'default' search engine shipped on Windows machines, and if you know nothing about anything, especially computers, you're just going to use what you're given.

I've asked a few of the 'older' people I know that I noticed were using Bing before now, "Why are you using Bing?"

The reply made me chuckle. "Is that Bing? I don't know... That's just the Internet".

I know I'm being facetious but the point is, that most people who just want to get 'online' and use the Internet don't really care too much about what website they're using to search for things, they just want to type their search in, and find the stuff they want.

It's all about the Likes and Shares, right?

Many people that I talk to are under the impression that if you don't take hold of Social Media in your business, you're losing out on huge profits and your competitors will win your potential business.

Other people that I talk to are under the impression Social Media is a complete waste of time, and are only interested in other strategies like Google or Direct Mail / Print Advertising etc.

So who's right?

Well, the answer is, neither and both. It's not possible to generalise Social Media on an overall basis, because the facilities and markets open to each Social Media platform vary.

For example, advertising on Facebook might bring you awesome results, advertising on another platform, no results.

Doing the exact same thing for the business next door in the exact same way, may give you the exact opposite.
I tend to summarise Social Media in the following way:

• It doesn't matter if you have 100 fans, or 100,000 fans on Facebook. It doesn't matter if you have 25,000 followers on Twitter. This alone, is not going to bring you a predictable or scalable stream of customers. That's not to say you can't *utilise* a big fanbase - but it's not where I'd focus your energy initially.

• It's rarer than you think to have content that goes viral. To force this to happen takes a huge amount of work and investment, and the ROI is extremely difficult to gauge.

• Making 100 tweets a day about your business will probably get you nowhere. Tweeting to people about how you can help them or some other reason to get them to opt in to your system may bring you further traffic – but has to be done in a careful and controlled way, otherwise you're just reported for spamming them.

The other question that I'm regularly asked is, "What Social Networks should I focus on?"
This is an interesting question and largely depends on your industry and more importantly your market. For example – you might think it's no good if you're selling consumer products to advertise them on LinkedIn, and to just look at Facebook instead. Well, let's look at business to consumer, and business to business, separately.

Business To Consumer

If you're looking to target an older audience, Facebook is a good place to go. It does have users of all ages, but really, the majority of the 'younger generation' will be using Instagram - so if you're looking to target a younger audience, Instagram is the place to be.

I focus my energies on platforms where I've got a consistent user base, and more importantly - a quality pay per click system - so that you can buy in targeted traffic. That means I would primarily recommend focusing on Facebook, even if you're going to advertise on Instagram, because it's all the same advertising platform.

i.e. You set up the ads on Facebook, and target your audience using their demographics, then let them run the ads across all the platforms.

In either case, whether it be Facebook, Twitter or Instagram, the key to success, much like with Facebook, is to get people *off* social media. Facebook has a very special, constantly evolving and insanely complicated set of algorithms in place. These mean that they only show the posts you make, to people they think want to see them.

This might be really frustrating to you as a business user on Facebook, but as a consumer, this is awesome. Some people moan, but in reality, with the number of pages they like and friends they have they don't really realise what their news feed would look like if they saw every post made by every page/person. For many it'd just flood their feed and they'd *miss* the valued posts that Facebook's trying to show them in the first place.

So how can you make sure your posts are seen by the right people?

OK... Now we're asking the right question... and I'll cover this more when I talk about Facebook specifically.

Business To Business

In terms of communicating to your customers, the most obvious platform is LinkedIn.

LinkedIn gives you the opportunity of connecting with people you've met very briefly (i.e. potential clients) and people that you're planning to meet. It's a great tool because you can arm yourself with a little bit more information before you meet them. Although if you don't want them to know you've been looking at their profile, you might want to pay to go Premium, then change your settings so that people only see "a person in X industry".

So why bother connecting to people on LinkedIn?

Being part of a professional network opens you up to communicating with potential customers more often. I have to confess I don't hold a massive value over it, and I wouldn't put any primary focus or efforts into building your connections.

But, as an example, if you have visited a client and connected to them on LinkedIn, you can send them a direct message to follow up on your meeting.

Your connections will build naturally over time – and it should be a tool that helps build on potential business, rather than being a tool to try and generate it - unless we're talking Pay Per Click to your website, and I covered that in the Pay Per Click section.

There are a few "obvious" things to both look at and talk about when it comes to LinkedIn. The most obvious is your profile page; have a look at it from an "External" point of view.

Isn't it boring? Have you just got your title as your job title? (Probably says "Director" or something else equally snooze-worthy).

Liven up your profile, and start treating it like any other direct response marketing piece. Create a desire for action; provide a call to action - whether that be to call you, to connect with you or to visit a web page.

Whatever your call to action - make sure it stands out and your LinkedIn profile will continue to bring you more leads.

Facebook / Instagram

Before I start - I've combined Facebook and Instagram as one. Not because they're the same site per se, but because we're going to be largely talking about Pay Per Click - and the Instagram Pay Per Click is all managed by Facebook.

So, years ago, I saw some people who had got amazing success with Facebook, and I mean amazing. I looked at their list size, and the cost per lead they were getting, and thought "WTF I want some of that".

Trouble is, I'd joined the party a bit too late. My CPC (cost per click) was quite high, and subsequently I struggled to get "big" list numbers. But the bigger problem I had, I also lacked confidence - which meant my headlines weren't particularly bold. In a place like Facebook you have to be bold to stand a chance.

To be fair over time I became more educated on the subject and I started to obsess over lead generation on Facebook. I started to generate a good number of leads from Facebook but I had a problem - I wasn't getting the take up on my services. Subsequently I didn't make an ROI from my spend, and I found it very hard to maintain spending at a loss continually.

So for quite some time, I stopped.

I knew it *could* work as a lead generating tool for a couple of very obvious reasons. One, I was seeing others get success. Two, it made sense. My target market *was on Facebook* I just couldn't reach them.

Another reason I knew it worked, in fact, was that I'd spent £1000's on stuff that's advertised on Facebook. From coffee to meat, from dog food to razors ... honestly, tons of stuff.

The meat in particular was a great example; it was from a butchers who had been advertising a lot. I'd ignored them for ages then suddenly just decided to click and read about them.

I've not bought anything from them recently but that's nothing to do with Facebook being the place I found them, it's to do with the fact that some of the meat I'd bought wasn't great quality.

And when you're paying a premium (which I was, a significant premium) you want quality.

Their service was pretty good and they dealt with my problems fairly well over the first couple of months, but I got sick of getting in touch with them over problems (a lesson there in itself, I'm sure).

But as I say, I've subscribed to coffee providers, razor providers (although not any more as I've opted for the "stubbly" look of late), and lots of other things.

So Facebook does work ... but it's like any other platform, you have to test, measure, refine, test, measure, repeat. Although I admit, for some time, I just ignored it and got in with marketing myself via direct mail, amongst other things.

But that doesn't change the fact that many marketers will tell you, Facebook is the way forward. I don't know when it all happened specifically, but I noticed a big change when I went back to marketing on Facebook around 2018. They had improved their AI and targeting tools, and suddenly I was getting a *far* better response rate.

So the marketers aren't *wrong* when they tell you social media and Facebook in particular is a great way forward, but I would warn over being told simply to build your likes and shares, and get lots of 'engagement'.

Yes that can be a good thing, but just like SEO you can't control it. Facebook can change everything in the blink of an eye and you've got no control over that. The real success for Facebook, comes in the form of the examples like the online butchers, where you're getting people off Facebook on to your own website, and getting their details or getting them to purchase something.

Or even better, selling them a subscription.

If you haven't got a Facebook account – get one. You don't have to put your real name or profile picture up there if you're worried, no-one will ever see it.

This is often the biggest objection I face when I tell people about it.

They 'don't want to be found'

Fair enough, but if you want your *business* to be found, get to grips with it, because it'll pay you dividends in the long run. And the main thing is, there are lots of people with the same name, so - if you don't want to be found, don't upload a profile picture and ignore any Friend requests; simple. No-one will see who runs your business page, it's literally there to represent your business - and that's it.

So you need to get a Facebook Page; don't worry so much about the Likes, we're not worried about how many likes your page has. We're using it as a base for your Ads, and in the long term, you'll build likes anyway as a side effect of the Ads.

But we really don't care about Likes.

Because things change so rapidly, I'm not going to go into huge detail here, and certainly no step by step - because the basics don't tend to change and that's what's most important here. With the Facebook ads, you get very fine control over the targeting. The main targeting options are:

• Location: you can specify a country, region or town and specify how many miles radius. This lets you make sure you can run your ads just to people in your area if you want.

• Age & Gender: as it sounds, you can specify the lower and upper age limit of the viewers of the advert, and whether it's men, women or both that view.

• Interests: this one is really interesting, this allows you to target on the fact that they like Golf, but they may not have actually specified that anywhere in Facebook – it's done purely on the pages they "Like" and the activities they do.

• 'Interested In', 'Relationship status' and more: There are many other filtering options which are always changing and improving. Make sure you take the time to read the rest of the options and target it any way possible.

In a nutshell, you can advertise very specifically with Facebook - and you can specify the platforms too, so if you just want to advertise on Instagram you can.

We also know that by determining our market, we can almost certainly find the right market to deliver our message to. Most people when they set up an Advert Campaign, want to get it seen by as many people as possible.

But I try to get it seen by as few people as possible, because the more specific your Ad is, the more profitable it will be. I would rather have 10 specifically targeted eyes looking at my ad than 10,000 untargeted.

LinkedIn

It's funny. For years I'd ignored the pay per click on LinkedIn because 'it's expensive' but ultimately, that's a stupid mindset. Yes, I admit, I was stupid.

I fell into the exact same mindset that the people I mocked in my section about Google did; forgetting that it's about cost per lead, or more importantly, *cost per sale.*

I'd looked at the cost per click and thought "pah, sod that".

But then some time ago, I thought: "I've got some cash to invest, let's try it". I invested a relatively small amount of money and started to get a huge amount of return in terms of leads, and that converted into good, solid sales.

At first I thought it had to be too good to be true and, whilst I had some initial conversion rates on the landing page that would make most Internet Marketers weep, they didn't hold forever.

But it still worked out as a 1000% ROI from the money I invested. Not bad, huh?

There are two things to say here … I didn't just rely on asking for someone's name and email and then wait for them to get in touch (a common mistake made by a lot of people doing Internet marketing).

I sent them emails, direct mail and I made phone calls to those that hadn't responded. The upshot is I generated sales and made a return on my investment.

Now there are scenarios where business to consumer, might work, and it entirely depends on what you're selling… but primarily - I'd focus on business to business with LinkedIn.

Remember, the secret is (still) to get them *off* the Social Media, whatever that may be, and on to your own site. Obviously it depends on the business but many people are far more likely to get away with visiting LinkedIn than Facebook during the day.

In some jobs it's even a requirement.

But that aside, what's really interesting is the advertising opportunities.

In a similar way to Facebook, you can really drill down on the targeting with LinkedIn, but it has a couple of really special features that you don't get with Facebook.

You're able to display adverts to people in a particular industry, with a particular job title or job function/seniority, by their skills, and even by what School they went to.

Advertising on LinkedIn is a little harder than Facebook, in that getting the click-throughs can be a lot harder.

And they're more expensive than Facebook, but generally the quality is better too. That is to say, if someone clicks they're more likely to engage. Remember to make sure you're sending the user to a highly specific landing page.

In my case, I tend to ensure the Google, Facebook and LinkedIn pages all are tracked separately. That is to say, if someone fills out a form on a LinkedIn landing page, when they enter the CRM (Client Relationship Manager, I use InfusionSoft) it 'tags' the contact with the appropriate source.

That way I can look at InfusionSoft, and see that this week 25 contacts have come from LinkedIn, 45 from Facebook and 100 from Google.

Print Advertising & Direct Mail

As business owners, I think it's fair to say - we've all 'been there'. The phone rings, and it's Steve from the local newspaper, magazine or some other popular advertising company. They have a 'one time' offer that if you run the ad today you'll save £250 and it'll be seen by 50,000 people. But wait, to get the most effectiveness, you need to run at least 3 ads, if not 5 because it takes a while for it to sink in before people phone you...

Well, after the first 5 minutes you were sceptical but after an hour of talking to Steve you're thinking this all sounds great, so you pay, run the ad and wait for the phones to ring. Because over 50,000 people will see your Ad.

After all, 5 Ads at £250 each, that's just £1250, and if 50,000 people are seeing it, and just 0.1% pick up the phone that's 50 people. If just 10% of that 0.1% bought from you, considering the gadget you're selling is £500, you'll have made £2,500.

And you're sure to get more than that, right? That's just the worst case figures. Right?!

But... the phones don't ring. Tumbleweed rolls by as you wait for the phone to ring. In fact, yep, you, along with a huge percentage of other businesses, have just been screwed by one of the most deadly approaches to advertising. Going for the medium first, then working out the message and not even focusing on the market at all.

Look at it this way - you should know your target market. Do you actually care how many people read your ad, really? (The answer is no. If you answered yes, think again.)

Look at it this way: The phones aren't ringing... and 0.1% is a tiny conversion rate, so why aren't people interested?

Well it's easy to compare - if you were selling high quality organic prime beef burgers, would you advertise them in a vegetarian recipe magazine? No, that would be crazy and stupid. But to an extent if you take the approach above, that's pretty much what's happening.

So how do you target your advertising properly? Well, the first answer to that is consider your market before your medium. If you're called with an Advert space for a great newspaper, question this first: are the people I want to reach going to be reading that?

Following on from that it's simple... Focus on the 3 M's (Market, Message, Medium) and you'll be on your way.

Remember, don't always advertise your product in the same magazine as your competitors just because you think that's the right place.

Test and measure, but if you're selling yachts, why not try a golfing magazine or similar? Think of your target market, then work out where they might be, then work out your message!

Of course, you could do the obvious thing, and do some direct mail instead. Let's just do a direct comparison. I don't think my figures above of £1250 are unrealistic for newspaper advertising, if anything that's cheap.

So take that same figure, and buy in a list of 200 people locally. That'll be under £100 if you go to someone like Experian. Then you could buy in some promotional products, and high quality paper, and print out some ads. In fact, you'll have a load of cash *left over* from a direct mail shot. You could probably do two or three highly targeted mail shots, for the same money.

So what form of Direct Mail works best? How do you go about it? Does the paper quality matter? Should you just send a letter? What about promotional products? What about telephone follow up?

So many questions.

What I'll share with you here is based on my actual experience of Direct Mail, alongside a ton of information I've read and absorbed from leading experts in marketing. The most important part of what I have just said though, is that I'm sharing this stuff based on actual things I've done… this isn't random opinion, it's based on experience.

It's expensive, right?

So many business owners completely dismiss Direct Mail these days. It's shocking, but understandable.

After all, if you can buy a database of 500,000 people for £350 and someone will SPAM them for £250 why would you spend £600 to send out a letter to a fraction of those people?

Well first, if you think the former is acceptable you have a bigger problem.

You should only ever send Email to people that have directly opted-in to receive it. That's not just GDPR related (it's still 'legit' to buy in a list and email them, they just have to be fully opted in to *that list*).

For two reasons. Number one, because Email is treated very differently to post, psychologically speaking. People are 'always on' with Email, and we all get a lot of really rubbish SPAM, so unless they've specifically asked for an Email from you, you shouldn't send it. But number two, because it can damage you/cause problems for legitimate Email marketing.

Another plain good reason for Direct Mail is because people are busy… and going back to the 'always on' attitude with Email it's quite easy to miss an email (maybe your email landed right whilst they were talking to an important customer on the phone, and they clicked on it, off it, then never went back to it).

Even if they're getting regular Email Marketing from you, they can go through 3-4 emails without really reading them. But when they get a letter through the post, it's pretty unlikely they won't even open it.

From a cost point of view, you shouldn't look at a campaign as a total cost anyway. You should be looking at it as a cost per lead or cost per customer. And as long as that cost per customer is lower than your lifetime value of that customer, you're doing well.

What Works Best?

Well, that's a very broad question which is very specific to your industry, your product or service, and where you are in your sales process.

One effective way to send the initial direct mail when you're really early in the relationship is to send using a postcard.

Postcards get a high readership simply because they don't need opening. There are quite a few sites out there that will provide the data as well as the print and send service – the benefit of that is you can design your postcard, work out who you want to send it to by area, then send out a mailshot. Or, you can upload a CSV (Comma Separated Values, basically a list of data) of your customers/leads you want to send it to, and then they will print and send it for you.

This is a great tool to promote an event or a specific call to action; if you're trying to encourage users to perhaps obtain a free copy of your report or guide, this is a great way to do it. Once they've made that interaction, that expression of interest, you know you can build your own list of who to re-market to.

Remember, the same rules apply here when it comes to engaging the reader. Make sure your headline isn't trying to sell something.

You want to attract attention to their problem, and how you can solve it.

What does your product do that makes their life easier?

Try to put yourself in their shoes – what is it that makes your product / service better than anyone elses? What is it that makes you the person to go to, and not your competitor who's actually next door to them?

Remember, even if you're giving something away for free – you still have to sell it.

You still have to convince them that whatever it is you want them to do, it's worth doing – that they would be making a huge mistake if they didn't.

Once you've started this process, you can refine your postcard format and send it out, area by area, testing the results each time.

Remember, they don't have to go to your website, they can go to "free-internet-marketing-guide.com" (ok that one's a little bit long – but the message is in the domain name itself).

It's often better, if you can, to set up a domain name that's relevant to the product/service/guide you're promoting.

Not only does it allow for campaign-specific performance statistics, but it's relevant and more memorable for the reader too.

Chapter Five:
Follow Up

I've seen too many people over the years (including people I've produced websites for) that decide once you've got your website 'online' that that's it. Done.

Your 'online marketing' is sorted.

Tick the box, move on.

But it's so much more than that. I know more people are getting more switched on to it now, simply from the number of people I speak to.

Businesses that 5, or 10 years ago wouldn't have touched Google Ads now have some sort of basic campaign running. But still, just running a bit of Google Ads to your website *isn't* sorting out your online marketing.

I don't get obsessed over everything being online marketing (as you may have gathered, by now) and you should still deem 'online' as one source of business, and no matter how many online sources you use to obtain new customers (i.e. Google, Bing, Facebook, Instagram, etc), you should group these leads as 'online leads' and have a good 'offline' marketing strategy.

So let's just cover the basics of follow up, and to reiterate my point before I get going – the follow up doesn't have to be *online*. It could, and should, contain some direct mail elements if you can.

So here's the scenario:

Someone's come to your website because they're looking for your product/service. They've found your lead magnet and opted in. They've given you their details in exchange for the promise of the lead magnet and agreed to follow up marketing.

The first thing I'd look at when working with online lead generation, is to prioritise the level/number of details you obtain for each lead. For example, what's the most valuable bit of information you need?

I'd argue, if we're talking about setting up an email campaign and regularly emailing, the most obvious answer here is email address.

I know a lot of really successful marketers who just get email addresses, they don't ask for any other information.

There's nothing wrong with that strategy and if your 'email game' is strong then maybe that's a good idea. But I'd still prefer to get their first name, and email as a minimum. I almost always ask for telephone number too but make it obvious on the form that it's optional.

But it doesn't have to end there, because once you've got their name and email, that's simply the first battle done. What you then need to do is try and ask for their direct mail address, or get them to schedule a call or similar.

So the idea of what we're building is called a funnel. If you imagine, at the top of the funnel, you have lots of visitors to your website. A number of those visitors will opt to give you their details.

And so, on the thank you page, they get an opportunity to enter their address for some other offer. A percentage of people will opt to do this.

Then on the following page, you can have an additional offer (perhaps to buy something, for an initial consultation, or anything like that). A percentage of people will opt to do that.

So at the top of the funnel, you have potentially thousands of people coming to your page.

At the bottom of the funnel, you have just a handful of people taking you up on your 'top level offer'.

The beauty of a funnel like this, is that it gives you additional opportunities for follow up. Right at the start, if you've convinced them just enough to go ahead and give you their name/email, but no further, then your emails can be driven to getting them to take the next step.

This is a crucial part of the marketing campaign that so many people just completely ignore. I've seen good marketers not do this, too.

Because it *is* effort, setting it all up. But you can set it all up and automate it, meaning once it's done, you can leave it running (my campaigns haven't been touched really, in over a year).

So let's talk practically, how do you do it?

One of the ways I do this is the first page I'll send you to offers you a guide, or a PDF of the first chapter of my book. Then, on the 'thank you' page, I offer you a printed copy.

So I start by asking for just your name and email (or perhaps even just email) but then quickly ask for your full address details.

If you don't give them to me in the first instance, the entire email sequence you're in, will encourage you to go get a physical copy of the book. After I while, I'll change the offer (because if that offer's not working it makes sense to change it up).

With a physical address you can combine follow up, so that for example, if you get a 'time limited offer' you can send additional information in the post.

So for example, I want to ensure that on the first day of the special offer, you get something in your email as well as through your letterbox.

The combination of mediums means that I'm much more likely to get your attention. I've picked up many clients with this strategy, and in fact one my clients called me, and left a message saying "Ben's been hounding me with stuff and I want to know what it's all about".

He'd been sent a load of chocolate, in the tail end of the campaign, with a final little offer. He took the offer, and over time became one of our biggest clients.

If people don't take up the offers I'm putting forward at the start, they simply then fall into my 'daily email' list. This is where I'll send out emails on a daily basis, which are conversational/entertaining emails (I'll give you an example in a little while).

Let's get to the REAL important bit here - the initial sequence.

It's not as complicated as it sounds, and it's really quite easy to implement.

So how does a sequence work?

Quite literally as you would expect a sequence to work. You set up a series of 10, 25, 50 or 100 emails (I run a sequence of about 45 for a 'cold' lead but I know people who run much longer sequences).

It's all completely automated, and so when the person first gives you their name and email, they then go into an automated sequence which sends them the emails you've set up, over the time period you've set up.

So just a simplistic example, you've got 30 emails pre-set, and they're set to go out every day. Joe Bloggs joins your list, and for the next 30 days gets an email every day.

This works for B2B or B2C – and as long as your emails are text based (i.e. conversational) and from a person (i.e. not your company name) and they have a solid call to action, you're on track to have a good sequence.

The argument for conversational vs newsletter format comes up a lot. One of my clients argued that their emails should be newsletter format because *that's what their customers expected.* But just because that's what's expected, doesn't make it a good idea.

Just take the typical example of looking in the newspaper, seeing how your competitors advertise, then copying them. You might think you're doing the right thing because 'that's what everyone else is doing'.

But just because everyone else is doing it doesn't make it a good idea; how do you know they're getting a return on that advert? How do you know they don't just advertise there for the sake of it?

The great Earl Nightingale said (along the lines of) "If you're in doubt as to what to do, look at what everyone else is doing and do the opposite, and you'll generally be OK". He's smart, you should listen.

But also remember, follow up should NOT be just one medium. Use as many mediums for the follow up as you can!

One resistance / hesitation I get when I talk to people about email marketing, is that they're worried they're going to be seen as spamming people, or that their emails aren't going to be wanted.

It's completely wrong.

What people don't like is irrelevant sales letters, newsletters or unsolicited email (SPAM). Can you really make use of email (and send emails every single day) to build a long-term relationship with a potential customer, who then might convert later down the line?

The answer is simple: Yes you can.

And before you say "That's fine, but it wouldn't work for my business", this works for pretty much *every* business. Even if you sell ice creams down the sea front, you could make this model work for you.

Build a list, build a following, and email those people to let them know when you're in their area. Have a special promo deal embedded in the email – and bingo.

More customers.

So where do we start?

Firstly, you should do a little segmentation. You don't always need to, for example, my daily emails go out to both new and existing clients. But you should be able to email just your existing customers, and just your new potential customers, or people that have expressed an interest in a particular product or service.

So for example, if I'm selling say, a website deal, I'll let all my list have the first email, but then if I'm sending multiple emails in a day (which I'll do when coming close to a deadline) I'll exclude my existing customers.

Incidentally, if you're segmenting contacts on an automated basis - remember to move customers from the potential list to existing list once they've converted!

The easiest way to build a long-term relationship is to tackle some problems in your industry.

"52 things to avoid when hiring someone".

On the landing page (the 'opt in' page, where they give you permission to email them) you give them 3 things to avoid and then "enter your first name and email here to get the rest". You can then have 49 further emails scheduled to send to them.

For this to work successfully, you absolutely must have an auto-responder. An auto-responder is something that allows you to pre-set emails and send after a set period of time – i.e. '1 day after joining the list', '2 days after joining the list', etc.

There are many auto-responder solutions out there, and for the non-technical there are some easy solutions. I have used a huge variety over the years, many for myself, for testing, and many for clients.

Because platforms come and go, and their features are always changing, I'm not going to recommend any one particular platform. Have a look at www.dbobible.co.uk and in the resources section there'll be some current recommendations.

Incidentally, I first realised this theory that 'you need email marketing software' about two years prior to writing this book originally. A year later, as I go over it again, I realise how fundamental it is. I genuinely can't see any reason why if you were looking to do any sort of email marketing software, you wouldn't set yourself up with a basic account from one of the big providers... the costs will be next to nothing.

Depending on where your lead has come from, you may or may not want to jump straight into 'sales' emails. I tend to avoid sales emails initially, as I focus on people looking for information, i.e. they're not in a position or prepared to buy - but you should still have some sort of call to action in there for the people that *are* ready to buy.

Overall, however, your email marketing should either be providing useful, helpful information that develops the fact that you're an authority on your subject, or provide entertainment.

Once they move off the sequence of emails, they then settle on your broadcast list.

Your broadcast list should be the place where they then 'raise their hand' to indicate interest in a product/service, are led to buy a product/service, or you simply "hit reply and get we can have a chat".

It's important to remember to keep your emails interesting. People engage with a story. Here's a good example - think about your time in School or College.

How engaged were you when your teacher/lecturer just droned out facts and figures? I know, from personal experience, this doesn't stick in your mind. I took a Computing A-Level at College.

Now it has to be said, I'm a reasonable fan of technology;

growing up I was hugely into every bit of technology I could get my hands on.

I knew how circuit boards worked, I even made my own sound card for a computer that worked through the parallel port. (Don't know what I'm talking about? Don't worry, just take me at my word that I was geeky).

Yet I got an E in Computing.

An E for goodness sake.

I had come out of School with an A* in GCSE IT, yet got an E in Computing.

And I was a geek.

How did this happen?

Well I can tell you, when I went to University, I had a lecturer who had a completely different teaching style. He was far more engaging, and you could say, perhaps in that one year I had matured a touch, but I took an exam in a module that was effectively exactly the same as the Computing A level I had essentially failed. (We're talking primarily Binary Maths here, if you're interested).

I got over 90% on the paper.

The same applied with Maths for me, actually. I was struggling at GCSE.

When I was around 15, my Maths, English and French were terrible; these were considered (obviously) as important subjects by the school I was in, and they insisted on removing me from German to give me extra lessons in Maths/English/French.

Now at the time, I hated them.

I suspect this actually festered a little over the years and I really disliked the school for it.

But *obviously*, they knew what they were doing.

I got given extra maths lessons with a different teacher, who again, had a completely different teaching style. He was more friendly, and interwove stories into his lessons.

The result? I went from failing Maths to getting a 'higher' B. (The 'higher' being the harder paper at the time, or something).

This is because, our minds are hardwired to respond to a story. This is exactly why no-one wants to hear about the facts/figures about your product. They just don't care.

But tell them about the time you did X when you were growing up, or you did Y last week and it was hilarious - they'll be far more engaged… and you just build in the sale at the end.

The Format (Geeky Stuff)

OK so we've got to cover a bit of the geeky stuff. Don't overlook this part, it's really important… and don't worry, I don't actually get that geeky at all.

The first thing I'd mention is fonts. You want to have your template set up so that it doesn't explicitly use a font, meaning it'll use the email readers' default font.

But one of the most critical points as I have mentioned before, about Email marketing, is that to get the best results from email marketing – you want your emails to be text based, i.e. conversational.

The email that lands in their inbox. It must look like it's naturally written. Just as if you'd send them an email from your email client. This means you want to strip out any extra HTML or rubbish from the template, so that there's no logo or borders, or anything fancy.

My point here is, if your emails land in the wrong format, or look wrong, they won't get read in the way that they should be.

"But everyone else is doing it…"

So why shouldn't you put your logo at the top? Or make the newsletter look attractive? Surely that's what the big companies do and so it must work?

I hear this a lot.

Especially from eCommerce companies, who think the only thing they should email out about is their products. But the thing is, it works for the bigger companies because they send out millions of emails every day. I can assure you that the type of email marketing that works more effectively than any other type, is you just writing an email as if you were writing to them from your normal email program.

Think about how many emails you get in your inbox every day.

You might only get a few but you might also get hundreds. I personally get hundreds every day, and every email that contains graphics in the middle of the email, nicely formatted (but missing massive chunks because I haven't downloaded images), is instantly regarded as a newsletter/commercial/junk email.

To be perfectly honest, because my email client doesn't download the images, I don't even read them.

By approaching the reader with text, you write to them in the format they are expecting to be written to in. This means that your message is far, far more likely to be read – if not, at least scanned very quickly, so if you make the text effective enough you'll capture their attention, and that's all you need to do.

What's the Frequency, Kenneth?

For those a little to young, that's a song by REM in the early 90's. I was listening to that track again recently… and for me it brings back all sorts of memories of our early family home.

Memories of, despite being the youngest brother, being the 'best' at computers in our family. Having huge aspirations of becoming an 'IT Man' from an early age (my love for IT has since faded a little - swapping out CPUs and fixing fans isn't as fun as it used to be).

It's funny how music can trigger such fond memories, this one in particular because it was on a cassette tape (ahh cassette tape... you know I had an apprentice who had no idea what that was... I think that makes me feel older than simply reminiscing).

This cassette tape got played a lot; normally when I was playing on or fixing our 'family' computer (which in the end was more classified as 'my' computer).

But bringing this back to email marketing: it's frequency that most business owners get wrong, because almost always they choose close to zero.

I'm not just talking about email marketing, but also how often you pick up the phone, write them a letter or arrange to meet up face to face. Basically, <u>how often you actually follow up</u>.

Practically speaking, the majority of those things (especially for the larger customer base) is just not feasible. Meeting face to face for example, wouldn't be practical for an eCommerce Business owner who sold thousands of products all over the UK.

Telephone calls can be expensive (although lucrative...).

The best way to manage a constant stream of communication is with email. And the best frequency? Well, I can pretty much promise you that whatever you're doing at the moment, isn't enough!

But here's something really important: if you haven't emailed your clients ever, and you suddenly start emailing them every day, they're going to wonder what the hell's going on. You have to ease into it if you're starting to email your existing customers (and make sure you're GDPR compliant, of course).

If you've got this big database of clients and you haven't emailed them in ages, the best thing to do, is send them a single email reminding them you exist.

If you start emailing on a relatively regular basis, you position yourself as regularly communicating to your clients. This in turn allows you to send more frequently.

In the long term you should be sending at least 1 to 2 emails a week.

It's OK If People Tell You To Go Away

You could get offended / take it personally every time someone unsubscribes. But - and this is what I do to be honest - you could also just quite simply not pay any attention to it, whatsoever.

Regardless of this though, you absolutely must send out emails using a system that will allow unsubscribes and that will monitor 'hard bounces' (i.e. email doesn't exist anymore).

One you've sent out that first emailing, (at which point you should be mentioning you'll be staying in touch more), you could probably start to email fortnightly. Once you've been emailing fortnightly for a while, you could move to weekly. Once you've been emailing weekly for a while, you could move to two a week, then three a week, then every day.

If you think people will get annoyed with your emails – look at it this way: they've got an unsubscribe button. If they unsubscribe, it just means they don't want your emails. It might mean they don't want to ever hear from you again, but it might just be they don't want your emails. It's not something to take personally.

"There's No Way I Could Email Every Day, Are You Crazy!?"

Yeah, probably, just a little bit crazy.

But am I crazy for emailing out every day? No way.

I had a reply from someone the other day that summed up for me exactly why I email every day.

Hi Ben...

I have to admit I don't always read your e-mails, some times I don't even open them... but every now and then I actually sit and read... Mostly it makes me think, some times I come away convinced that I'm still heading in the right direction... Phewww... and every now and then I just enjoy the time off to read what happening with you ... so keep up the good words and hope the book gets done soon

Mark

I often get replies along those lines, although very often they also include an enquiry for doing some business. That is, if they haven't followed the call to action.

But it very much describes the reality of the situation. By emailing frequently and being entertaining and engaging, you're constantly in peoples minds. So when they finally decide to make that purchase, whether it be for a Website or a Takeaway Dinner, you're the one they think of.

I don't know what to write...

The thing is, it's like most things. The more you do it, the more proficient you get at it.

I wouldn't say I was a 'natural writer'. Back, many (many) years ago, I was able to waffle on in things like course work for School/University, but there's a difference between waffle content, and concise, engaging content that drives a call to action.

This has been learned only by a lot of reading but frankly, even more practice. I've written a daily email practically every day for the last six years. That's a lot of content, and a lot of practice.

One big concern I hear often about email marketing, and sending regularly, is "there's only so much I can say about XYZ". It's true, there *is* only so much you can say about your own business / industry / product / service, before it becomes boring.

But there are ways to talk about what you do without being boring. What you don't want, are emails filled with facts, figures and charts and every statistic under the sun. Because no-one really wants to read all that, do they?

Whilst I'm sure that one of the best features of the Buggy 2000 is that it's got "Ergonomic Foam handles" I'm not sure I really care.

Maybe if you said "This buggy will be easier and more comfortable to hold with these ergonomic foam handles" I might be slightly more interested/captivated.

My point is, don't just list features and copy specifications or product guides. If you were in a shop or marketplace or wherever you sell, and you were talking to someone, selling to them face to face (or over the phone...) - what would you say?

You probably don't realise some of the best sales copy you could ever write comes out of your mouth on a daily basis.

In fact, even better than that, if you're telling friends/family about your product/service, how would you describe what you do, to them?

When it then comes to your regular (whether that's fortnightly, weekly, or daily) emails, write your emails like you're talking to a friend in the pub...

Things like perfect grammar and English are less relevant (but not entirely irrelevant, in fact regular sloppy mistakes make you look pretty unprofessional) but the key here is you want to formulate your email like you're talking to that person.

Because you *are*.

You're talking directly to the reader; you're not talking to a list. Let me say that again, because that's so, so important. You're talking directly to the reader; you're not talking to a list.

Where Do You Get The Time?!

This is, again, something I hear a lot. The thing is, the physical writing of my daily emails takes around 5-10 minutes, generally. Sometimes it can take longer, and sometimes I'll write 2 or 3 in one go if it's a particularly big story.

When I started out, it would take an hour. It would feel forced, uncomfortable and often very difficult - but over time it got easier and easier.

It's like anything. When you start, it'll be difficult, or unfamiliar. But give it a few months of doing regular emails, and you'll not even really think about what you're writing.

In fact, you'll find that things will crop up during the day, or you'll think of something whilst in the shower, and you'll chuckle to yourself and say "that'll make a great daily email".

I frequently pull stories out of my head that come from childhood, and very often they can quite easily tie into what I'm selling, but if not - you just end it with "and whilst I'm here I must remind you to get this gadget…".

To prove the point, here's a complete example of one of my daily emails:

Hi Ben,

I wouldn't say I was a particularly rebellious child growing up. I adhered to the rules pretty much at school.

I was lucky in that I went to a 'decent school'. Having passed my 11+ I was inline to follow my brothers to a Grammar School in our area. I have to admit I don't know that I enjoyed all of it, but then who does?!

Anyway... I'm pretty sure this was in Year 9, because I'm sure my "Partner in Crime" was Year 11 and I know I was 2 years younger than him... So that would make me around 13-14.

This wasn't Steve though...I don't think he was involved..(but he might have been, this is going back a fair bit...). This was someone else, equally geeky as I recall. He must have been because I'm pretty sure he wrote most of the program, although I know I had my fair share of input.

For any fellow geeks on the list, bear with me if things seem simplified, but I'm aware not everyone will care about the technical details....

So what did we do? Well, being young teenagers keen to "rebel" in our own way (the geeky way) we thought we'd have a go at the "IT manager"...(if you could call him that....). He was always deleting our copies of games we had carefully hidden... rather rude if you ask me... Anyway, we had observed, in our own awesome way, that every time the PC booted it erased all the data from "T drive" - a shared network drive that was effectively on the server.

Wouldn't it be funny to put something on that drive that meant it would take ages to reboot?? (Well, to a geeky teenager then, the answer is Yes. I appreciate the answer might be "Why?" now...). But that wasn't taking it far enough... no... We'd determined the best way to cause havoc, would be to create loads of data on each PC then reboot them all it would take ages to boot up to Windows. Hilarious I tell you...

So how did we do it? Well, we wrote a program to do it. We did it in a VERY simple coding language intended to teach us the basics of programming, and basically made it create a folder on the drive with random characters and letters. Doesn't sound too complex no? Well, the funny bit is, because we used random special characters, Windows wasn't able to delete them. We knew the techie would probably have a little bit of trouble with that...

In order to not get caught (clearly an important factor here) we decided to run the program under 1st Years logins. How did we guess those? Easy. Go to the sports board, find all the kids in the football club (you KNOW they wouldn't have reset their password) and go login with their initial and last name, and password of "password".

It worked like a dream. On our last count we'd created over a million folders on each PC. We rebooted all PCs and went off innocently to our lessons. It worked maybe a little too well though. It didn't just slow them down, it totally broke them. Nothing worked, at all. Dead. Oops...

On a break a little while later, I was with said partner in crime. We were going to go to the computer room, but, well it was down (how inconsiderate of someone?!) so we went to the technology block, as the PCs there weren't linked to the main network.

On our way through the main door (and this noise echoing around the school entrance will last with me forever):

"WATERS!! (and someone else here)"

(I've removed the name of the other person... but that's the other guy I did this with...). I don't ever recall seeing this teacher (the head of IT...with the "IT Manager" sat next to him...) angry, either before or since this occasion.

Ah. Something wrong sir?

We had performed I guess what you could really refer to as a

School boy error...We had run the program under the 1st years accounts so untraceable, but oops, we'd left the original source code in our own home directories.

Sigh.

Needless to say, there was (well deserved) punishment, Saturday detention amongst other things...plus we had to write the antidote (which really wasn't hard, but I feel that was more of a point of principle).

We had a lot of fun with that School Network / Computer system...and the story of the Technology Block Computer Room must be saved for another day...

...no real sales message here, just an amusing story. Last chance to book my final slot for a meeting on Monday by the way...remember, your competition will almost definitely have given up for the year now - so don't hang around, make 2014 a great year and do it on the back of a solid marketing campaign!

Kind regards

Ben

PS. After the initial meeting with the teacher we were sent off to the headmaster. We were made to feel very sorry for what we'd done. Funny though, if it was me in his shoes, I'd do the opposite. If they'd recognised we'd actually achieved something pretty cool at the age of 14/16 and harnessed on to that with encouragement/stronger IT focus (this was the mid 90's so hardly likely) who knows where our programming skills would have ended up.... anyway, have a great weekend (after you book this meeting)!

That was from quite some time ago, and I can't remember the

exact response of that one email, but I know the emails I sent within that 2-3 week period on the run up to Christmas/New Year generated me quite a few meetings, which in turn generated a substantial piece of work in the New Year.

In terms of time - that one email took perhaps 20-30 minutes to write, because I was simply writing about a memory, something that happened to me. And when you're effectively telling a story of something that happened to you - the words can flow quite easily.

And yes, I know it's not grammatically perfect, but that doesn't matter. It has an impact, sure, if it's ridiculously difficult to read because of spelling/grammar, but it mostly doesn't matter (and I'll explain why in a second).

If you're still not sure how to get started, then there's one tip I can give you, as was given to me by my mentor – before he was my mentor.

Write Like You Speak

I remember being on Jon McCulloch's email list – and right at the start in about the tenth or so email, it said "go watch this video and then come back".

I did as instructed and within a few seconds chuckled, as I realised what he'd done. He'd dictated the email. So when I went back, the words that were in the whole email were literally what he'd said. Clever.

Considering we all walk around with a Dictaphone equivalent these days (i.e. your smartphone) there's no excuse to not getting started.

But there's an added benefit to writing like you speak. Not only does it make it easier to read, it automatically injects your personality in to your writing. There are, for sure, more formal ways I could write this book.

I've written this entire book like I'm having a discussion with a friend, or colleague. Being realistic, that scenario probably includes the pub.

So not only does writing like you speak enable you to get writing instantly, but it also means that you're starting to do all your marketing 'right'. You're injecting your personality into your marketing and that starts to polarise your audience.

They'll either love you, or hate you.

I frequently get either emails telling me I'm just plain wrong, or emails calling me extraordinarily rude words.

I find both amusing. Firstly because the ones telling me I'm wrong are expressing their unwanted opinion, and it's completely unfounded. I have been doing this for years, and I know it works. I also have it from great authorities on the subject, that it works.

So I'm not taking the opinions of *Joe Bloggs* who's only involvement in email marketing has been reading various newsletters from various lists he's on.

Maybe he sends his own newsletters, and maybe they work. That doesn't mean conversational email wouldn't work *better*.

Secondly, the ones demonstrating their breadth of knowledge in the English language also amuse me. Because they've essentially had an emotional reaction to something I've said and want *me* to deal with it.

That's not how it works.

The reason I mention all this, is that when you're doing this you must be prepared for some 'backlash'. Because you're not going to be loved by everyone.

"If you haven't pissed someone off by noon, then you probably aren't making any money." - Dan Kennedy

It's not about being obnoxious, and it's not about swearing in all your email content. It's simply about expressing yourself, injecting your personality, and saying what you believe is true.

In my instance, I tell people the 'right' way to do a lot of their marketing, and I explain how to do that in a lot of my emails. Many of my emails simply contain opinions, or stories, but the essence remains.

As such, you're either going to love being on my email list, or hate them. The good news is, for each person that ends up hating you, and unsubscribing... that's one more person who's been brought closer to you.

Follow up is such a critical part of a campaign's success for this very reason.

Of course, it's not just about email. I've talked about, in various parts of this book, when you get details of people you want to get the maximum number of details you can.

Ideally, you want their name and email at least. But if you can, get their phone number, and their address. Any additional details you need that are relevant for your product/service are a bonus too.

I have a variety of campaigns, and each one of them has a variety of follow up options. Take just one as an example, the 'free book' campaign.

I ran this on a variety of platforms and had great success with it. It's as simple as it sounds.

I run an advert, offering my book for free. I'll put it in the post and pay for everything. You literally just give me your address.

As an offer, it's quite strong (as long as the book is relevant to your audience, obviously). It means I can ask for name, email, address, phone number and will likely get pretty good opt in rates.

So here's the bare bones of the campaign:

- Someone sees an advert for the book, clicks.
  - They don't fill in the form, they see adverts reminding them they can still get their free copy.

- They fill in the form, and I tell them the book will be in the post shortly, but I also send them an email with the first chapter.

- I send the book out, in a gold shiny padded envelope, with a bar of chocolate.

- They get a series of 32 emails, over 28 days. The last 3 days emails are a 'hard sell' for my marketing services.

- On the first day of the final 'hard sell' they get some more chocolate in the post, with another sales letter.

- On the last day of the final 'hard sell' – they get a phone call.

The latter points obviously assume they haven't made contact first. Some do, some don't. But as a campaign overall, it worked. I don't tend to use that particular campaign any more for no other reason than it's 'evolved'.

That was originally, from around three years ago. I sometimes consider starting it all again now, and I might well do, but the model I work with as I write this, was given to me by Dan Kennedy, and I like that model better.

There are a number of really important things you have to consider when you're looking at your follow up. I've talked about it all a lot, but let me summarise.

First, you need to keep your content interesting, relevant,

informative and/or entertaining. Content can never be too long, but it can be too boring. I'm on the list of quite a few marketers, and quite a few send via conversational emails.

There's more than one that I don't even bother reading any more, because the emails are frankly – a bit boring. At least, I guess, that's how *I* find them. His other readers might be thrilled by the content, I don't know… but I doubt it.

Second, you must always have a good, strong call to action. Without this, everything you're doing is weaker, and almost destined to fail. Don't get me wrong, sending emails and follow up is better than nothing, but people need <u>direction</u>. They need essentially telling what to do.

Make sure your content tells them what to do.

Third, is make sure you use a variety of platforms/mediums. We all get thousands of emails every day/week. More so now than ever before. We've grown accustomed to it, and for many of us it's second nature to have 13,451 emails in the inbox.

Standing out with email marketing is hard. That's why your email should always come from a person, and it should always be like it's written *to* your lead. That way they'll be far more likely to read the content in the first place.

But if you can combine follow up with telephone and direct mail, you'll get a far better response rate. A good example, is a campaign I ran, I ended up following up on the phone to my leads as well as sending more marketing via the post. I was selling my membership group *Creative Tribe* and combining telephone and direct mail, I got 5x the sales on the last couple of days.

Without your follow up, a campaign such as Google Ads, or Facebook, simply won't achieve its true potential. You'll join the ranks of the hundreds of thousands, if not millions, of other business owners who say: "I tried Google, but it doesn't work for my business".

I'll finish by saying, if you want more resources, and examples, and to watch some free videos on marketing, and pretty much everything I've talked about in this book, simply go to:

www.dbobible.co.uk

Chapter 6:
Recommended
Reading

Writing this book, I've been influenced by a great number of authors and professionals. I probably *could* list it out in a proper 'bibliography' format, but most people aren't *really* interested in that, are they? So instead, I thought I'd list my top recommended books. These are the books that have helped me grow my business the most over the last decade or so.

"The 80/20 Principle" by Richard Koch

"Switch: How to change things when change is hard" by Chip and Dan Heath

"Work The System" by Sam Carpenter

"The 12 Week Year" by Brian Moran

"NO B.S.: Direct Marketing" by Dan Kennedy

"NO B.S.: Time Management" by Dan Kennedy

"Grow Your Business Fast" by Jon McCulloch

"Promo Power Supremacy" by Mo Yusuff

"Profit First" by Mike Michalowicz

"Ultimate Sales Machine" by Chet Holmes

"Influence" by Robert Cialdini

"Self-Publish Your Book And Become A Respected Business Author" by Bill Goss